Green Mama is pure gold. I love this book not only because Tracey Bianchi offers practical "green" tips that any busy family can tackle, but also because, whether she's dishing on eco-snobs, confessing her own eco-sins, or sharing her dream of green churches, readers see the heart, mind, and funny bone of a woman who loves her family, loves her God, and loves this earth he entrusted to us..

CARYN DAHLSTRAND RIVADENEIRA, author of *Mama's Got a Fake I.D.*

Green Mama is a clarion call to live more responsibly. I haven't read a book in decades that has more profoundly affected the way I live.

ARLOA SUTTER, executive director, Breakthrough Urban Ministries

Tracey Bianchi's *Green Mama* reminds us that we are to care deeply about God's creation. It starts by opening our eyes to the easy, yet important, eco-possibilities that come our way every single day.

ANITA LUSTREA, executive producer and host of Moody *Midday Connection*

I'm a little ticked at Tracey Bianchi. With only a modicum of guilt, she sucked me into caring about her "green living" campaign using humor, common sense, and God's Word. Now I'm eco-examining everything and, in the process, considering becoming a "green papa."

MIKE MURPHY, director of spiritual transformation, Breakthrough Urban Ministries; associate pastor at Christ Church, Oak Brook, Illinois

Tracey Bianchi has written a lovely, accessible, family-friendly book on living green. Grab a mom friend and introduce your tribe to the fun it can be to care for planet earth.

ADELE AHLBERG CALHOUN, copastor of Redeemer Community Church, Wellesley, and author of *Spiritual Disciplines Handbook*

Green Mama offers the ordinary mom an accessible model and guide to a greener lifestyle. With humor, storytelling, and grace, Bianchi pushes the activities and ideas of being "green" beyond what is simply trendy, offering a realistic way to honor creation and teach our children to do the same.

SHAYNE MOORE, author of *Global Soccer Mom*

Tracey carefully weaves the holistic message of creation care, our lives, and Christ's model with honesty, humility, and an edge of humor that pulls the reader out of complacency. In *Green Mama*, Tracey illustrates the real impact each mom can have on her family, her community, and her world.

DR. LIZ SELZER, director of leadership development and events, MOPS International

Tracey Bianchi is no environmental softie, but neither is she a messenger of ecological doom. Humor, honesty, and humility grace the pages of this creation-care primer, where Bianchi ties even the grittiest practicalities of green diaper choices and sustainable birthday parties into the wild and sublime narrative of God's love for his creation.

KENDRA LANGDON JUSKUS, managing editor, *Flourish*

Informative and engaging, *Green Mama* is, simply put, a good read. Tracey Bianchi is a gifted storyteller who explores the impact of her choices, ever seeking to walk more gently on the earth.

JENNIFER GRANT, journalist and mother of four

Having spent time with Tracey in the Colorado backcountry, I can attest to her commitment to creation care and environmental stewardship. Such a long step from her first bumbling trip in the wilderness of Washington.

BRAD WIDSTROM, assistant professor, chair, Department of Youth and Family Ministries; and director, Outdoor Leadership Focus

Green Mama is filled with theologically sound, practical, and guilt-free ideas for those who wish to join her in not only honoring God by caring for his creation, but also raising a generation who will present the gift of our limited resources to future generations.

DR. LARRY LINDQUIST, assistant professor of Pastoral Ministry and Evangelism, Denver Seminary

Environmentalism can seem preachy, meddling, and self-righteous, pointing out all the fun things you're not supposed to do. Come to think of it, so can religion. So how does Green Mama Tracey Bianchi manage to combine them while avoiding finger-wagging and tut-tutting? By letting grace and kindness infuse her call for all of us to rediscover what it means to be truly human, experiencing nature, family, and God's goodness to the fullest.

RUSTY PRITCHARD, husband and father of three; president of Flourish: Creation Care for Churches and Families, flourishonline.org

This highly practical book will inspire you with great, doable ideas that will change how you drink, eat, shop, dress, vacation, decorate, parent, play, and think.

CARLA BARNHILL, author of *The Green Bible Devotional* and *The Myth of the Perfect Mother*

As a stressed-out mom of toddlers who cares deeply for God's creation, I appreciate Tracey's utterly doable approach to God-centered green living.

JULIE CLAWSON, author of *Everyday Justice*

green MAMA

The Guilt-Free Guide to Helping You and Your Kids Save the Planet

Tracey Bianchi

WITHDRAWN

ZONDERVAN®

ZONDERVAN.com/
AUTHORTRACKER
follow your favorite authors

ZONDERVAN

Green Mama
Copyright © 2010 by Tracey Bianchi

This title is also available as a Zondervan ebook. Visit www.zondervan.com/ebooks.

This title is also available in a Zondervan audio edition. Visit www.zondervan.fm.

Requests for information should be addressed to:
Zondervan, *Grand Rapids, Michigan* 49530

Library of Congress Cataloging-in-Publication Data

Bianchi, Tracey.
    Green mama : the guilt-free guide to helping you and your kids save the planet /
Tracey Bianchi.
        p. cm.
    ISBN 978-0-310-32036-4 (softcover)
    1. Sustainable living. I. Title.
GF78.B53   2010
640—dc22   2009040178

All Scripture quotations, unless otherwise indicated, are taken from the Holy Bible, *New International Version®, NIV®.* Copyright © 1973, 1978, 1984 by Biblica, Inc.™ Used by permission of Zondervan. All rights reserved worldwide.

Scripture quotations marked TNIV are taken from the Holy Bible, *Today's New International Version™. TNIV®.* Copyright © 2001, 2005 by Biblica, Inc.™ Used by permission of Zondervan. All rights reserved worldwide.

Scripture quotations marked MSG are taken from The Message. Copyright © 1993, 1994, 1995, 1996, 2000, 2001, 2002. Used by permission of NavPress Publishing Group.

Published in association with the literary agency of Alive Communications, Inc., 7680 Goddard Street, Suite 200, Colorado Springs, CO 80920. www.alivecommunications.com

Cover design: John Hamilton Design
Cover illustrations: Veer and Artparts
Interior images used by permission. Copyright Art Parts/Ron and Joe, Inc.
Interior design: Beth Shagene

Printed in the United States of America   *Printed on recycled paper*

09 10 11 12 13 14 15 • 23 22 21 20 19 18 17 16 15 14 13 12 11 10 9 8 7 6 5 4 3 2 1

For Charlie, Danny, and Lilly.
And for Liz, the greenest mom I know.

Contents

Acknowledgments

I never really understood how much effort it took to put together a book. Every time I flipped open someone else's story, I would see this fancy little section where the author would gush over her friends and family. She would thank them for the support, the prayers, the edits, the encouragement. I confess to naively thinking, more than once, *Is it really that much work, or are authors just overly dramatic?* Now I get it. My friend Adele, when I told her about this project, said to me, "Well, I don't envy you." She'd just finished a book.

Without dear friends and family surrounding me through this process I never would have dreamt this up, let alone put my fingers to the keyboard. Friends like Suanne who read every page of this manuscript, offering honest, sometimes gut-wrenching feedback and lots of love the whole way. It's your turn now, my friend. I love doing life with you.

I am also so thankful for Amy, Nancy, Donna, and Suanne (again), the small group that nurtures my soul, and for Lisa G. who always said she was not doing enough to help me but did just what God had set aside for her to do, read what she could. For Koilia, the best little manuscript group on the planet. For Erin, who always told me I should write and never stopped saying it. For Lizzie B., Megan, Nana, and Shawna, who hung out with my kids so I could pull this off. For Liz, my deepest green friend, from whom I learned much.

You were an inspiration for this book. For Kate and Adele, I miss you both and love you from far away; your belief in me means the world. And for the great folks at Zondervan and for Beth, who took a chance on this first timer.

And I am thankful for my family. For my mom and dad who taught my sister and me how to camp and who insisted that we always "play outside." I owe my love of the outdoors to them. And I am thankful for their constant encouragement and their support of this endeavor. They've always been in the front row cheering me on. And for my sister, Nikki, who sat next to me in the car on every family vacation. My childhood was better because of her. I love you and miss you so much, sister (and my cool Forest Service brother-in-law, Eric, too).

Thanks to Lisa, and Grandma Sandy (the very, very best mother-in-law) for reading along. And to Christine for getting half her office to sign up for my Facebook group! For the rest of my famiglia, especially Grandpa John, Frank, and Sal. This book is also for their children Salvatore, Stella, and Isabella, my nieces and nephew. This is your planet and I hope we can all save it for you.

And of course, I am thankful for my ever-patient husband who gave up so much time and energy so that I could write this book. Your consistent love and support means more to me than you will ever know. Your wisdom and ability to always ask me the right questions (even if I did not want to hear them) has shaped my heart and mind in many ways. I love you so much, honey! And finally, most importantly, I am thankful for my three children. The most fantastic, adorable, hilarious, witty, brilliant, and beautiful trio. Charlie, Danny, and Lilly. Mom loves you! This book is for you. May your souls someday feel the breath of God brush your cheeks from the highest mountain peaks, and may you see God's reflection in the puddles at the park. This is your book and your planet. I pray we can make it a better place for you.

Why I'm a Green Mama

The conspicuous consumption of limited resources has yet
to be accepted widely as a spiritual error, or even bad manners.
BARBARA KINGSOLVER, *ANIMAL, VEGETABLE, MIRACLE*

The earth is the Lord's, and everything in it.
KING DAVID, PSALM 24:1

After graduation from college, before diapers and the drama of sibling rivalries were my everyday, I flew to Seattle for a long weekend with some friends from work. We had decided to try our hand at backpacking on the Olympic Peninsula. It sounded impressive, and it was high time I had an elaborate-sounding adventure like this. So we marched off to our local mountaineering shop to buy backpacks, new water bottles, and more gadgets than a band of girls in the backcountry would ever need.

One of my traveling companions had an offbeat and unflappable brother named Ed who was lucky enough to live in the Pacific Northwest. He was a crunchy sort of guy, the type I imagine George Clooney might look like were he mixed with the wilderness side of John the Baptist. Scruffy and standoffish, yet impressive and almost dapper. Ed, it turned out, was a very accomplished climber and mountaineer. He was also leading our novice expedition. And he was completely irritated with us.

The morning we left for our excursion, he watched as we over-stuffed our packs with food from the local market. Lots of pasta with red sauce, energy bars, crispy snacks, and of course, Diet Coke. Nothing says backcountry like aspartame. Our packs were plenty heavy, and by the time we had hopped a few ferries and arrived at our starting point, I was ready to motor back to Seattle. Getting situated at the trailhead took us a while. We wobbled like newborn calves, lifting our gear to our backs, swaying under the weight. Ed stood aside, cool and detached. He and his small pack had been ready for half an hour. Eventually we were ready too. We needed to march in just a few easy miles before dinner, but as we dipped into the wilderness, I was already silently gasping for air and fretting over my pending blisters.

That night, we set up camp and sat in a circle like delinquent Girl Scouts. Giggling and clutching plastic bags filled with spaghetti sauce, we fiddled with our pots, hoping to boil enough water on our single burner backcountry stove for two pounds of pasta. We guzzled soda, blathered on about our new headlamps, and formulated an elaborate dessert plan. Meanwhile, Ed quietly chewed his simple meal of lentils in a cup. After dinner, we sloshed soapy dish water all over our campsite. I noticed that Ed did not clean his cup but instead made some green tea and drank it out of the same gooey mug. Later he brushed his teeth, swirled the last of his cold green tea—lentil mix around in his mouth, and then swallowed it.

It was gross.

It was also called Leave No Trace camping. A stealthy way of spending time in the backcountry, taking great pains to make sure no one knows you were ever there. The idea is simple. Leave the wilderness the same, if not better, than you found it, so those who come after you can enjoy it. As Ed rolled out his sleeping pad and his makeshift tent (a tarp and a string), ants drifted in to dismantle the piles of marinara and M&Ms we dispersed during our spastic supper hour. While he settled into a comfy slumber, we traipsed off into the woods to brush our teeth and take care of business. We left broken branches and toilet paper in our wake. The evening ended in our turquoise tents complete with card games and of course, more snacks.

We were a disgusting mess, and we were definitely leaving a trace.

How I Got from There to Here

That trip proved an amusing but cringe-worthy memory. Entering the wilderness that August afternoon, I had no clue how obnoxious, cumbersome, and cloddy I was. I operated under the naive assumption that I could shop like crazy, eat whatever I wanted, and could even pack it all into the backcountry if that struck my fancy. I could trash the earth with self-centered pursuits. I could trash my body with whatever tasted good. I was completely oblivious.

The fact that my consumer habits and my daily cup of coffee were leaving a permanent scar on the planet, on God's creation, had never occurred to me.

My journey into green mothering started on this trip. Granted, I was a newlywed at the time and seven years from children, but something about the way my friend's brother moved through the woods, but also through his life, motivated me. I will admit that slugging down toothpaste and lentils was not super-exciting, but his example of moving gently through this life was. The more I thought about it, leaving things better than I found them even started to seem, well, a little like something Jesus would do.

The years have zipped past, and I find myself domiciled in the suburbs with three kids and no backpacking adventure in sight. In the intervening time, I've learned how to travel a bit lighter and discovered that reducing the physical impact my family makes on this world can enhance the spiritual impact we have. A few ideas from Leave No Trace, mixed with the ever-growing green trend and a whole lot of Jesus, have landed me in a place where I recognize that how I live matters greatly to the planet, to my children, and to God. And it matters for you too.

A Few Caveats

The Green Mama Project that you hold in your hands is the story of tweaks and changes I have made to my life over the years. Some were surefire winners and others are still works (and arguments) in process. I have been captivated by the transformation of my heart and soul along the way and find that I am desperate to share with anyone who will listen, and often with people who won't.

I lecture helpless baggers at the grocery store on the sinister side of their plastic bags. I inundate my husband with propositions for bamboo flooring and low-VOC paint. I irritate my mother with talk of organic strawberries. I'm growing greener every day, and I absolutely believe that doing my part to save the planet is also following the call of God on my life. So I wanted to share my journey, with the hope that you will find yourself in the throes of a little green revolution of your own.

All of us will create our own unique version of a more sustainable life. The exact details largely depend on how committed we are to this movement, the time and energy we have to implement changes, where we live, and what is most important for our own family. For example, moms in rural communities may have access to wide-open spaces, and moms in agrarian communities may know considerably more about planting that organic garden than the urban mom. Urban and suburban moms likely have access to programs and mass-transit options that rural moms may not have. Where you live can play a significant role in defining what green living looks like for your family.

For some families, sustainable living might mean downsizing to a smaller house, purchasing more from secondhand shops, selling a car, or concocting a home remedy for common ailments. For other moms it might mean heading out to buy organic cotton sheets and ten pounds of fair-trade coffee, or a commitment to take the train or light rail system to work. Every mom can create her own unique definition of green.

The Suburban Caveat

My version of green comes from my life as a suburban mom. It is what I am. For years I have wished I was something else, perhaps a chic urban mom living in some snappy loft. Or better yet, a mom on an organic farm with hippie friends to sit around and sew with. Other times I long to be the sort of sturdy mountain mom who cross-country skis to the grocery store.

But it is the suburban life for me. I'm happy to say I live in an old community, in a house nearing 100 years of age, and I can see the Chicago skyline from just a few blocks over. From my front door I can walk to the bus or train. I am just minutes from one of the busiest airports in the world, and twenty minutes from downtown Chicago. This metropolitan area, according to the 2007 census, boasts about 9.5 million people, and I am one of them. Smack in the middle of the country, smack in the middle of the suburbs, smack in the middle of chain restaurants and SUVs. The number of Americans living in urban or suburban areas hovers around 80 percent, so I am definitely not alone.

These details will help you understand where this book is coming from. Where I live, materialism reigns supreme, and living a life of moderation rarely occurred to most people until the economic debacle of 2008 forced them into it. And I am a Midwestern suburbanite, which means I am cold for six months of the year and I can get to a mall much quicker than I can get to a trailhead. So you will find an emphasis in this book on resources and ideas to help navigate responsible living and thoughtful consumption with a suburban flavor.

The Green Caveats

Some of you may find me greener than you want to be. The ideas I toss out may prove themselves bigger modifications than your family will make. You may write me off as a hippie girl who needs to get out of the trees and into a minivan. You may imagine me growing all our food in the backyard or bicycling everywhere, but we are a family of five, and I drive a station wagon. I only bike for fun, and my kids love fruit snacks, so, much to my chagrin, we snarf down high-fructose corn syrup like the rest of the nation. I also still highlight my hair.

Others of you will find me not green enough. There are thousands of green ideas, and I've left out quite a few. Life with kids is hectic. There are fabulously green people who have authored books on how they ate locally for a year, grew their own food for a year, or said farewell to their automobile for a year. These people are my heroes! But I am not moving or giving up my car anytime soon. Three generations of my family live where I do, my husband's job that pays our bills is here, our friends live here. This book is a look at green living from this place; it is for those of us who are desperate to change things but are not packing everyone up, uprooting good community ties, and heading out to elsewhere just to be greener. You will not find a chapter that covers every detail of climate change or a political call to environmental activism, a rally against GMO's or even seven steps to composting success. These issues are important, but you just cannot cover everything.

I hope we will meet someplace in the middle, where the best of a greener life meets the reality of your everyday. And as we wade through the rapidly growing options for eco-friendly living, I hope you will see that a sustainable life is in fact God's hope for you, and how we treat this terrestrial ball called Earth is a reflection of how we view God.

If your most treasured friend gives you a necklace for Christmas, you treat it well. Maybe it is not your size or style, maybe you don't love everything about it, but this gift represents her attempt to love you. So you care for it. It's the same with God's planet. As we care for it, we honor God by respecting the gift he gave us. Creation is one of God's many ways of loving us.

The Jesus Caveat

Several of you have picked up this book because you wanted to learn more about the green life and all this God talk is making you nervous. I'm okay with that. There's no hidden agenda here. I am simply sharing my green journey with you, and when it comes to saving the planet, I cannot separate the cause from the Creator of the world.

Some may consider this a bit naive and misguided. I am okay with that too. I happen to believe it is rather bold. Elizabeth Barrett Browning once wrote, "Earth is crammed with Heaven, and every common bush afire with God." Our green journeys are crammed with heaven indeed. So if you come to this book a bit skeptical about the God part, as we journey together you may find that the ordinary details of the natural world are really a glorious invitation to dance with God.

One More Reason: The Eighth Commandment

Over the years, I've had the audacity to look at God's Ten Commandments and skip over a few that I felt I had nailed down. I'm not prone to cheating on my spouse, I'm not at all considering killing anyone, and I take a nap on Sunday. I thought this was true for "thou shalt not steal" as well, since I'm not given to snatching stuff.

I know something dramatic, like stealing a car, is just one extreme example of this command, and that tying the commandment to the idea behind it is really the issue. But I had never once thought deeply enough about this commandment to link the heart behind it with the issue of ecological integrity.

That was until my senior pastor, in a thought-provoking sermon, pointed out all the little ways we steal every day. He defined *steal* as simply taking more than your share of the resources. Stealing is not limited to grand theft auto. There are a limited number of resources in this world, and when we take more than we need, simply put, we are stealing from others. We can do this in a variety of ways— financially, socially, and environmentally. By pillaging the earth for more than our share, we break the eighth commandment. We steal from our children. We steal from their children. And if the planet makes it that far, we steal from their children too.

Barbara Kingsolver writes that our arrogant, take-what-you-can-get lifestyles are not really as free as we may think. "We get [them] at a price. Most of that is not measured in money, but in untallied debts that will be paid by our children in the currency of extinctions, economic unravelings, and global climate change."[1] Our lavish lifestyles come with a price tag, and we are brazen enough to think they are really not all that extravagant, when compared with, say, Donald Trump. So we steal from our kids in seemingly benign little ways. Like sneaking little bits of their fresh air with gas-guzzling SUVs (but at least they have a DVD player on board), building our dream home on what was once an apple orchard or prairie (but at least they have more space to run around inside). And we steal from other children when we miss the fact that across the world it took another child's labor to make our $1.99 flip-flops. This has added up to an overloaded debt to the planet that we can no longer pay back.

I snatch more than my share of resources all the time. Once I journeyed into green mothering, I felt quite proud of myself and naively thought I was getting the hang of it. I owned reusable bags and napkins. I turned off every light switch I could; I shopped organic; I conserved water. Then I took a survey that revealed how much stress my lifestyle still placed on the planet. After calculating things like my use of electricity, water, and how many times a year I fly, the survey showed that if everyone on the earth lived the same lifestyle that I did, we would need the resources of three planet Earths to sustain that behavior.

To my dismay, I realized that even in my own, sort-of-green world, I was stealing from people, present and future. Turns out I constantly steal from my kids (and yours). I'm snatching up goodies like clean air and water while millions of families clamor for a drink and struggle with disease. I'm throwing away excess paper and packaging while rain forests disappear. I'm a kleptomaniac. But I am determined to address my failings.

I am thankful that you are reading along. Not because it sells books (actually, I hope you borrowed your copy, because that saves resources), but because if we all become just a bit more aware of the stress our lifestyles place on the planet, we can actually manage the damage before our kids inherit a trash heap. If we all take a few small steps, we can keep the creation God designed for us to enjoy available for this very purpose. You can be, as they say, an agent of change, even if all you manage to do is start recycling your aluminum cans. As with so many lessons in life, the smallest steps (even when they come under the weight of an overstuffed backpack in the Olympic Mountains) can eventually lead you to the greatest adventure.

1

Wisely and Well:

Teach Us How to Live

Oh! Teach us to live well!
Teach us to live wisely and well!
Psalm 90:12 MSG

Earth provides enough to satisfy every man's need,
but not every man's greed.
Ghandi

Craning my neck, I looked out the back window of my car and zipped down our driveway. We were off again for another morning preschool loop. My toddler whined for his pacifier, my infant daughter had already tossed her rattle to the floor, and my preschooler wanted gum.

As we merged into morning traffic, my then four-year-old gazed out the window and asked, "What does *important* mean?"

Always hyper about an educational opportunity, I threw the question back at him. "Well, honey, what do you think it means?"

He grunted, not impressed by my savvy parenting, and explained that he did not know, which was why he asked in the first place. So I started rattling off a list of important things: family, friends, God.

After a few tries, he got into the game, and we bantered back and forth: his brother, his bed, his blankie.

As we pulled up to a stoplight my son's eyes must have been drawn to the park on the corner, ringed by enormous trees.

"Mommy, do you know what else is important? Trees are important," he said.

My morning caffeine jolted me into a giddy chatter. "Yes, yes, yes," I cheered from the driver's seat. Indeed, trees are important. After years of coaching and cajoling it seemed my son was destined to start Greenpeace for Preschoolers.

I am a self-proclaimed tree hugger. I recycle like a mad woman. I think camping is God's gift to the overcivilized. I honk at people who whip fast-food wrappers from car windows. Plastic makes me panic. Trees are important! This was the sort of statement I'd waited four years to hear.

"So, honey, why do you think trees are important?" My waiting eyes darted to the rearview mirror.

My darling son paused, and then said thoughtfully, "So they can catch on fire and we can chop them down."

My heart slid to the floor mat as he droned on about firefighters and logging trucks, the things dear to his manly little heart. Apparently impressing the value of God's creation on my children would require more than a few bedtime stories and wishful thinking.

The Green Life

Living a "green" life (one that emphasizes caring for the earth's people and resources) is all the rage. Flip on HGTV, and you will find people building and remodeling houses with green products. Chances are your local newspaper offered several articles on green issues this year. In my community a group of realtors now bicycle together on home tours. And Googling the words *organic cotton* will leave you inundated with catchy T-shirts and baby onesies that proclaim to the world your witty commitment to all things earthy.

This stewardship (care taking) of the earth, both ecologically and socially, is an issue that lies deep in the very heart of Jesus. Phrases like "climate change" and "sustainable resources" did not exist two thousand years ago. Jesus' disciples never supported organizations called the World Wildlife Fund or the Sierra Club. Fancy blue recycling bins did not adorn the streets of Rome.

Yet long before Al Gore, Cameron Diaz, and a cadre of other celebrities made their mark on environmental and social issues, Jesus shared the passion God has for this world: passion for the poor, the defenseless, and the needy, passion for the wild places, the rivers, and the mountains he created. God starts out with this story actually. It's the first thing we read when we crack the Bible open — God's amazing act of creation in Genesis 1. God was the first environmentalist, Jesus the original humanitarian.

And this planet is a way for us to know something about God. In the book of Romans, we read that "since the creation of the world God's invisible qualities — his eternal power and divine nature — have been clearly seen, being understood from what has been made" (1:20). Which means that our majestic mountains and ice blue lakes, our acres of forest and even our dandelions are a display of God's power. Who are we to dare to trash that?

For those who follow Jesus, sustainable living is particularly gripping because it reminds us that all of humanity is called to compassion, wisdom, and stewardship of all forms (see Luke 16:1 – 13; Gen. 1:26). I am passionate about following Jesus, so this invitation to stewardship pulls me out of my overabundant life and into a different reality. It reminds me that crashing through the giant super-mart and flinging everything from diapers to deodorant into my cart, without thinking about who made them and what happens to them once I'm finished, does not honor what I know to be true about God.

Genesis tells us about the creation of the world, culminating with the creation of man and woman, and then this amazing mission for them: "Rule over the fish of the sea and the birds of the air and over every living creature that moves on the ground" (Gen. 1:28). If God created this world and then invited the last of his creation—human beings—to help look after it, then I have a responsibility to lavish on this earth more green wisdom than I currently do.

Lawson Younger, an Old Testament professor I once had, said that what the Bible does not say can be as important as what it does say. When it comes to the way Jesus lived, the Bible never says that he owned a four bedroom colonial or did his best to grow his financial portfolio. He was not seen wasting resources or trashing the landscape where he walked and lived. He was a minimalist, only taking what he needed for his journey through this life. He encouraged those who followed him then to do this, to live simply, and he invites us to do the same today.

Sustainable living is absolutely doable. It is possible, even for overworked, often frantic families like mine. If labeling your family "green" feels somewhat new and ambiguous, just dip into your past. You might find this lifestyle crop up in a few unexpected places. My husband and I were not raised by organic farmers or ex-hippies, but our parents exposed each of us to the splendor of God's creation as young children.

I spent my share of summer vacations on the lumpy floor of a canvas tent in Montana and on the shores of the Atlantic Ocean. My newborn bottom was diapered in cloth; it was the only option available for my mother.

My grandmother was a product of the Great Depression, and with a deeply ingrained fear of hunger and scarcity she reused everything. She had piles of old rubber bands, plastic bags, and straws all over her house. She kept paper napkins, reused disposable doilies, and even took leftover butter pads home from restaurants. To this day,

I've never met another person with an ability to preserve and reuse everyday items the way she did. She never labeled it eco-friendly living, just common sense.

In my own life, I remember the special moments when my mom handed my sister and me our very own ice-cold glass bottle of Coca-Cola, complete with the crown cap. It's the sort of idyllic, all-American memory that feels like some commercial. My sister and I would smile, gulp down a bubbly swig, and then, indeed, we wanted to buy the whole world a Coke. I also remember taking all eight of these glass bottles back to the grocery store and turning them in to be reused. Not recycled but actually reused. Cleaned and refilled by the Coca-Cola Bottling Company.

The current American obsession with disposable everything was unheard of just fifty years ago. Church picnics never generated the piles of paper plates that they do today. Grocery aisles devoted solely to throwaway food containers did not exist.

Even our national fascination with bottled water is a recent fad. It began in 1989 when water companies began bottling with plastic. This landfill legacy is now an $11 billion – a-year industry but is a trend barely twenty years old.[1] So if we look back to the way our grandparents and even our parents raised us, we will find many tips and tricks for green living that we already know.

An eco-friendly life does not demand that we overhaul every aspect of our family's life. For many of us, the wisdom to live wisely is already rooted in our family tree.

A Sustainable Life Is Within Your Reach

Green is the color du jour, and we are surrounded by people, whether they practice a faith in God or not, pursuing God's plan for this planet. The number of green programs, resources, and organic products is larger than at any time in recent history. And if you cannot grab greener ideas for living from your local market or library, the internet is pulsing with green tips and strategies for reclaiming wasted items, gardening, recycling, repurposing, and rethinking how we live. Maybe for the first time ever, wise moms like you have easy options to save the planet with and for your children.

I know this whole green life can come off as a bit overwhelming and even snobbish at moments. Rest assured, I am not an eco-snob. I am an overtired, hypercaffeinated, stressed-out mom. I have a busy life, and green options need to work smoothly for my family, or there will be anarchy. Sure, I have visions of grandeur wherein I drive my car on vegetable oil and pull my family off the power grid, but these are just dreams for now. My dear husband still rolls his eyes at more than half my ideas. And, like almost all my greening mommy friends, I have been known to forget those reusable bags at home!

I'm a woman in the throes of parenting three young children, and each day the intricacies of raising them fills me with tremendous joy and grates on my nerves. Yet despite the chaos, each day I still manage to take a few green steps. You can too.

This book does not demand impossible changes for your life. You do not have to compost every banana peel, ditch your microwave, or convert to organic gardening to make a difference (although these definitely do help). You do not need dreadlocks or a hemp handbag.

Instead, let's look at the simple solutions that make the biggest differences. Like this one: Americans toss 60 million of those plastic water and beverage bottles into our landfills every day.[2] There is a cheap, family-friendly, and even money-saving solution for this plastic problem: Drink from a reusable bottle.

You can do this.

You can repurpose your summer play dates by giving kids clean, empty, squeezable ketchup bottles for water wars (and they work much better than many squirt guns). You can turn your car off instead of idling outside the school while waiting to pick up your children (research suggests that if you are going to idle more than thirty seconds you will save emissions if you shut it off). You can wash your clothes in cold water and save 1,600 pounds of carbon dioxide emissions in just one year.[3] These are tiny tweaks to your way of life that can add up big for your kids, the planet, and even your wallet.

You can do this.

I've heard it said that there are different shades of green. Families come in every color. You may find yourself dark green in a solar-powered home or pale green with a couple of recycling bins. Green living is not a contest to see which family can compost the most. Every effort no matter the size or shade makes a difference.

What Matters Is That
You Do Something

The weight of saving the world does not rely solely upon you. God can save the planet himself. Actually, he already has, which is tough for me to swallow because I like to think God needs me. Ultimately, God is interested in your heart and movement toward wise living and responsible stewardship, not how many gallons of water you saved this month. He created this world and then invited us to partner with him in caring for it. He wants us involved in the process, just like I want my children involved in the projects I design for them. Of course I can make the chocolate-chip cookies myself (and, honestly, it would be so much easier that way), but I want my kids to learn how to measure and count, and then I want them to practice patience as they stare at cookies through the oven window. Their hearts and minds are transformed in the process. We learn magnificent truths about our Creator when we care for God's creation. This is what God wants for your family when it comes to taking care of the earth. The trees and the mountains are bursting forth with God's goodness (see Isa. 55:12). This is good for our souls.

The prophet Moses prayed to God, "Teach us to live well! teach us to live wisely and well!" (Ps. 90:12 MSG). I think this is a brilliant prayer. My deepest hopes do not concern my children growing up happy or content but growing up wise.

Living wisely and well means that our children learn to make God-honoring decisions with their resources. It means they discover how to see through marketing hype and the slick packaging of our culture so they can make solid, planet-friendly choices regarding how they live and move through this world.

This is wise living.

Chasing fireflies, walking to the park, everyday conversations, prayers, and trips to the grocery store can be opportunities to teach your children the importance of God's planet. You have the privilege of nudging your children toward wise living when you help them fall in love with the beauty of this world from the Amazonian rain forest to the anteaters at the zoo.

After my son finished waxing eloquent about setting trees on fire, I realized again how hilarious and unexpected this road of parenting can be. My car that day carried a modest canvas school bag, reusable grocery bags, reusable stainless steel sippy cups, and a reusable travel mug. And one pint-sized lover of the logging industry. No amount of reusable material could convince my son that trees in the parks were for keeping. Sometimes, despite your best efforts, the lesson does not stick.

Your kids will not go green by staring at their reflection in your coffee mug. Just like with karate or guitar, they learn best by doing. They watch you, learn a few tips from you, and then set off on their own. If your home is filled with earth-friendly choices, chemical-free food, and the chance to get outside and play, your children will grow up healthier and will be more likely to seek out a similar lifestyle for their own families. Wisdom is a gift to pass down through the generations. So dig out that travel mug hiding in the back of your kitchen cabinet; turns out it makes a difference.

What Does God Have in Store for You Today?

Each day as I wade through the disaster that my house has already become by 8:00 a.m., I sip my coffee and wonder what God might have in store for us that day. Every morning in the fog of mothering it takes a conscious decision to make wise choices for my family. Will it be another afternoon of errands, the mall, whining, wanting, and clamoring for more out of this life? Or will there be a moment when we purposefully live with wisdom and notice the peace of God glimmering in a puddle, streaming through the trees, or dancing on the grass? Will we be part of the problem or creative advocates for change? What does it take to raise children with a heart for others and eyes for God's creation?

When the conservation movement started, most followers of Jesus shrugged it off. Rather than embracing organizations aimed at preserving God's majesty and beauty, many churches have ignored these issues or sloughed them off as the obsession of mountain town liberals. Conservation efforts and Christianity often did not play well together. But we've reached a point in human history where we are running out of resources, and, as with everything else, paying lip service to the ideas of Jesus without acting on them gets us nowhere. It's not a liberal or conservative agenda. Giving our children a healthy future should be every parent's agenda.

As a mom I've used the cliché that I want to give my kids the world. This has meant that I want access to winning sports teams, snappy uniforms, good schools, college scholarships, and a wide assortment of friends, youth pastors, coaches, and teachers to dote on them every step of the way. It did not really mean that I wanted to give them the world.

But it should.

If you can help them learn to save the world, then you can truly help give them the world. I want my kids to have the heart of Jesus for this planet. I want to give them God's vision for this earth. I want them to live wisely and well. I want them to know that the trees are indeed important. My hunch is that you and I have at least this much in common.

Green Steps

At the end of each chapter you will find a few tips and ideas for your family to try. I call them Green Steps because an eco-friendly life is accomplished one small step at a time. These green living options can help all our families walk farther down the green path. Pick just one idea at a time from the green steps section, or choose one resource from earlier in the chapter to implement for your family's life. Start small. It's a big world; don't exhaust yourself.

1. Explore the eco-examen.

For centuries thoughtful people have discovered God's guidance for their lives through a series of simple questions called the examen (known as the "examination of consciousness"). The examen is a way of tapping into our daily experiences to find the "God moments" that helped shape that day. Several families I know do the examen on a regular basis. It has many different names, "ups and downs" or "highs and lows." Simply put, the examen is a way of asking "for what moment today am I most grateful? For what moment today am I least grateful?"[4]

Before bed, or at a good stopping point in our day, I ask my oldest son, "What was the best part of your day?" and "What made you sad/angry today?" It is a fascinating window into your child's world the way he experiences it. Quite often what I assume are highlights were not even on his radar screen. In the regular asking of these two questions, I have discovered everything from his favorite flavor gum to the real reason he cries at gymnastics.

An Eco-Examen is asking these simple questions with an eye for the natural world. You can make these creation-oriented adaptations part of a daily examen or something special you do on vacation or after a trip to the park or zoo. Your questions might include:

What was the best thing you saw outside today? What was one thing you did not like?

What makes you happiest about winter (or spring, summer, fall)? What do you like the least about this season?

Where in nature did you feel connected to God today? Where did you feel disconnected?

Where did you see beauty outside? Where did you see damage or destruction?

2. Adopt an examen for this book.

As you sift through this book, you will find more ideas than you can immediately implement, so consider taking an examen approach to this book. These are good questions to work through with a small group or book group. At the conclusion of each chapter, I'll ask you one version of two simple questions:

What is one thing from this chapter that you want to implement for your family?

What is one idea that you will not be putting into action anytime soon?

Do what works for your family. Consider the rest and feel the freedom to set aside what does not work.

3. Learn.

Check out the green scene in your community. Many libraries and community colleges offer guest lectures or ongoing courses on green living. Joining a classroom full of other eager learners will help you download tons of green wisdom in a short amount of time. One-time green classes often crop up around Earth Day in April. Keep an eye out for them.

Log on to the internet for some great eco-tips. *National Geographic*'s Green Guide (www.thegreenguide.com) and www.treehugger.com are two good places to start.

Your local museums can be another source of green information. Many offer exhibits on green living, and local botanical gardens and children's museums usually offer kid-friendly gardening and local ecology courses.

Finally, thoughtful retailers and grocers may offer newsletters that educate consumers on everything from wind energy to organic strawberries. If you have a local green grocer or mountaineering shop in your community, start there. National chains like Whole Foods, Trader Joe's, and REI also offer green living tips through newsletters as well as an occasional class. If these are not available near you, consider checking the library for a few resources, such as:

> *Earth in the Balance* by Al Gore (New York: Plume, 1993)
>
> *Garbage Land: On the Secret Trail of Trash* by Elizabeth Royte (New York: Back Bay, 2005)
>
> *Serve God, Save the Planet* by J. Matthew Sleeth (White River Junction, Vt.: Chelsea Green, 2006)

4. Read chapter 1 of Genesis.

As we start our journey toward a greener life, it helps to remind ourselves of how this whole adventure started. The book of Genesis in *The Message* reads like a story and will help settle your soul into

God's design for our planet. Find a quiet moment or pull your kids aside before a hike or a nature vacation. Read this text and take a break every few sentences to look around. Sometimes we separate ourselves from Scripture and miss the fact that the very trees swaying in our backyard are filled with the leaves that dance in God's creation story. Take a moment to let it sink in that God's thumbprint is alive and moving all around you.

5. Take the first step.

Finally, try these easy-to-do paper-saving opportunities as a way to get started:

Stop unwanted junk mail and catalogues from coming to your door (www.dmachoice.org).
Stop phone books from arriving, and agree to get your information online (www.yellowpagesgoesgreen.org).
Cancel your newspaper and magazine subscriptions and read them online, or share copies with a friend who also subscribes.
Avoid printing out emails.
Recycle or reuse the paper that you do use.

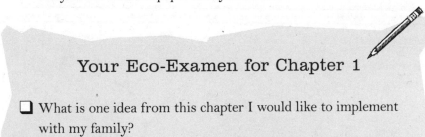

Your Eco-Examen for Chapter 1

❑ What is one idea from this chapter I would like to implement with my family?

❑ What is one idea from this chapter I am unsettled about trying?

Your One Big Thing:
Think Big, Start Small

I Am Woman, I Am Invincible, I Am Tired ...
BOOK TITLE, PETER PAUPER PRESS

Think globally. Act locally.
VARIOUS SOURCES

Every morning the headline news for the day includes details of some local or international catastrophe. Media groups and our Web browsers pry open our hearts and our minds with stories of mudslides in California, earthquakes in China, and tsunamis along the Pacific Rim. The moment we fire up our laptops or televisions, we are pulled into these stories. Over the phone an endless string of charities are also vying for our attention. Eager volunteers call at dinnertime to request clothes for their homeless shelter and donations for the new community center. If I scan the magazine rack in a checkout aisle for even thirty seconds, I am inundated with warnings of climate change and eroding wildlife habitat all over the world.

It's all a bit much if you ask me. I care deeply for these pressing issues, but this truckload of need dumped on my family each day is draining, a state of constant overload that has been dubbed "compassion fatigue." It is both a state of mind, as Susan Moeller tells us, that has been hyped up by the news media as well as a legitimate diagnosis offered by mental health professionals. Compassion fatigue, simply put, means that a person is just too exhausted by all the options to care about any of them.

In the wake of September 11, some caregivers and rescue workers found that a cloud of numbness and indifference settled down on them. Therapists reported that these individuals showed mild interest at best in areas where they once had great passion. Compassion fatigue was the diagnosis for their listless behavior. This syndrome is a reality found in many caring professions as well as in relief workers and on the mission field.

It also happens at my house.

I'm an overeager optimist. My husband knows to brace himself when he comes home from work because in a single day I might sign us up for dinner with a lonely family and a charity fundraiser (both on the same night). All I need to do is scan the church bulletin, and I am suddenly teaching Vacation Bible School, working at the local food pantry, and going on the high school mission trip (all in the same week). If I see a homeless person on the way home, I add serving the local homeless to my list. Before bed I will read up on the AIDS pandemic in Africa as well as the latest statistics on our disappearing ozone. I'll check my email one last time and find an update on vanishing rain forests in Brazil.

All in the same day.

So Where Does a Wise Family Begin in This Massive World of Need?

My friend Suanne once told me about her desire to help women pinpoint a single issue in this world that moved them so deeply they could not help but get involved. She wants to help moms focus their often disjointed energies so they can be sharp agents of change. She calls this her "one big thing" and defines it as the point where your passions and God's heart for this world merge. It is the place where you find yourself unable to sit still, sleep, or give your brain a rest. Bill Hybels calls this his "holy discontent." The apostle Paul says that God began a good work in us and will see it through to completion (see Philippians 1:6). We've got big things inside of us that need to come to life.

If I am honest, I will confess that, because the options for helping others are so vast, at times I just decide not to care. It is easier. Recognizing my one big thing prevents me from slipping into an overwhelmed, apathetic indifference. It helps moms like you and me discover one issue or campaign we can throw our energy behind, instead of scattering it everywhere like goldfish crackers on a play date. It can keep our families in the action at a level that allows us to make a significant contribution rather than write off the whole mountain of good causes.

My friend Amy is an example of this sort of targeted do-gooding. She has a daughter with special needs. Whenever she meets a new mom overwhelmed by the fact that her newborn child is unique in an unexpected way, Amy leaps to action. Her heart naturally overflows into the lives of these women. Using her own experience, she casually coaches and talks them through the rough start of their mothering journey. She is not a professional therapist or a social worker. She does not head up a nonprofit for special needs children. She is simply a mom who found her one big thing, and she makes a difference there whenever she can.

When It Comes to Saving the Planet, What Is Your One Big Thing?

A greener life asks you to find your one big thing for God's creation. What ecological issue moves you to action? Do you fidget at the thought of losing the habitat of an animal your kids adore? Do children lacking access to clean water sources stay on your mind long after the heart-wrenching commercial is over? Does the smog layer over your city usher your asthmatic children inside on an otherwise lovely summer day?

What is your one big thing, and how will you make an impact on that issue?

As you begin to extinguish the anxiety that stems from trying to do everything, you will be able to focus on just one thing. Study it. Pray about it. Learn about it. Act on it. This sort of thoughtful change is within your reach. This sort of discernment will help us all turn a deeper shade of green.

The Giraffe Exhibit

One spring morning I hauled my children to our local zoo. After wrestling with the diaper bag and misplaced zoo passes, we hastily forged ahead to our favorite place: the giraffe exhibit. Immediately the air was filled with the shrieks and squeals of a toddler overcome by his desire to climb into the giraffe habitat. Since no amount of rational explanation could curb his sudden penchant for giraffe cages, as soon as we arrived at the exhibit we exited with everyone pitching a fit.

I was cranky and completely worn out by the reality that at this rate we would never get the hot pretzel I was craving. As we fled the giraffe exhibit, we stumbled past an old safari Jeep, perfectly placed to make me feel as though I were hauling my kids across Tanzania. My oldest son pointed and asked, "Mommy, whose Jeep is that?"

Exasperated and suspicious that this was the first in a string of fifteen questions my frayed nerves could not handle, I sharply answered, "It belongs to a poacher."

Of course, he innocently asked, "Mommy, what is a poacher?"

"Someone who kills the animals. Now come on, honey, let's go."

He gasped.

Instantly reeling with guilt, I attempted to soothe over my sharp retort with lame explanations about poachers, the ivory trade, and endangered animals. Because poaching is a real issue that threatens our world, I spent the rest of the day unleashing my own version of compassion fatigue on my son. We shuffled through our zoo morning with heavy hearts.

Then I spotted a simple flyer with a tip for helping children save the planet. The words stopped me in my tracks: "Your kids need to learn to love the earth before they will want to save it."

First Comes Love

Before your child's one big thing becomes traipsing off to Swaziland on a campaign to save the white rhino, she needs to fall in love with the white rhino. Before she will know what her one big eco thing is, she needs to fall in love with God's world.

As moms we can easily transfer our compassion fatigue to our children. We so desperately want our kids to care about this world that in our earnestness, we can smother them with too many harsh facts that their innocent minds cannot comprehend.

So before we fret about the demise of the white rhino, let's learn to love it first. And how can you love something (or someone) without knowing something about it? So here goes: Did you know that most white rhinos spend twelve hours a day eating, eight hours a day resting, and the other four hours socializing (a perfect distribution of time if you ask me)? White rhinos spend significant amounts of time wallowing in mud to cool off and weigh anywhere from 3,000 to almost 8,000 pounds.[1]

These are just the sort of facts any kindergartner would certainly deem fascinating.

White rhinos are cloddy, cumbersome animals that kids can easily adore. The cognitive leap from lovable to huntable is too daunting for the mind of a young child, so freeing your kids to simply fall in love with an animal is the first step toward saving it.

There is plenty of time to learn that there are only two subspecies of the white rhino remaining. That, according to the World Wildlife Fund, the northern white rhino teeters on the brink of extinction. To be exact, there are only four northern white rhinos left on this earth. Just four. (Sadly, the African Rhino Specialist Group reports that these four have not been seen since 2006.)

All are in the Garamba National Park in the Democratic Republic of the Congo. So, basically, the four remaining animals live in a country ravaged by civil war, where people's daily fight for their own lives makes protecting a rhinoceros seem quite irrelevant. Your children can learn about these shocking facts later.

For now just take them to the zoo and work on saying *rhinoceros.*

One Big Adventure

Whether it is saving the white rhino or accomplishing whatever lofty goals their minds conjure up, as moms we dream big things for our kids. Tucked someplace in your mind you probably have several outdoorsy dreams to which you want to expose your children.

Do you want them to swim at a lake you splashed around in during your own childhood? Are there mountain peaks you want them to summit? Do you want them someday to scuba dive off the Great Barrier Reef, to know the difference between a field sparrow and a song sparrow, or to see Denali National Park?

Write these down.

Find a journal, type them into your phone, or tuck them in your Bible.

Just be sure to jot them down.

Throughout my life wonderful teachers and mentors have encouraged me to find a prominent place to make a note of the goals I have for my life. My friend Shawna makes a top ten list every January first. People make reminders to pursue what is important so when life gets messy and their vision gets cloudy, they can find their focus again.

Write down the eco-goals you have for your children. Perhaps you never thought of them this way, but chances are you have desires that they visit certain places or even accomplish something as whimsical as learning to climb that oak tree in your backyard.

So next time my eco vision gets blurred and I find myself guzzling gasoline on a needless trip or tempted to shop out of sheer boredom, I will remember that while I have been to Maui and Maine, my kids have not, and I want these places to be there so my children can experience their grandeur someday. If I could choose the adventures for my children, I would want them to ski the Canadian Rockies, work in Colorado for a summer, and hear a glacier calving off the coast of eastern Alaska. I also want them to learn the names of the prairie wildflowers native to the Midwest where we live. And I want them to hike up to the snowfield on top of Kilimanjaro before it melts (which is predicted to be gone by 2015). For many moms I know their list holds things that are close to home and across the world. Wherever your heart leads you is the place to start.

For example, my own mom donates to the preservation of local farm fields near her house so that urban sprawl does not invade her community and steal the landscape. She wants her grandchildren to visit her home and see open land the way she does today. Another friend talks about her children hiking and biking around the 300 acres of land in Pennsylvania that her parents own, and still another wants her son to someday ice-climb and backcountry ski the same wilderness she does today.

I want my kids to be in places like these because the very heart-beat of God seems to thump a little louder when I'm standing in ankle-deep saltwater as the sun slips into the ocean. I want these places to remain intact so that my kids can feel God touch their skin with the salty, sticky sky on a deep autumn night. I want their souls to sense the intensity of his presence in the places on my list. Keeping in mind the adventures we want for our children will help us determine where to invest our eco-energies, and it will help your family discover its one big thing.

I keep a list so that my one big thing includes efforts to preserve these places, since every one of the locations on my list is eroding. If we don't change our lifestyles, these destinations will pale in comparison to what they were when we first fell in love with them, or worse, they will vanish completely.

Mountain Pine Beetles

For many years I ignorantly thought my campaign for the planet was optional. In my mind I had committed to change, but my daily life did not seem affected by disappearing reefs or eroding shorelines. I read about these issues but naively assumed I would never sense their loss. My life is comfortable. The trees in my front yard are big, our grass is green, and I've been to my share of backcountry destinations, so I never really expected to suffer the consequences of any looming ecological disaster.

That was until I planned a recent trip to Colorado.

Chattering away on the phone like middle school girls, my adventurous friend and I planned our next rendezvous. In denial that my body had changed after birthing three children, I begged her to take me mountain biking and suggested Winter Park, a well known adventure sport community.

She gently said no because it was now heartbreaking to visit that area.

The formerly deep green mountainsides that drew millions of visitors to this community are now mostly dead and brown. Millions of the lodgepole pine trees in Winter Park and throughout the Arapahoe National Forest now poke up through the dirt like dry twiggy sticks. An infestation of mountain pine beetles is boring its way across the western United States. Predictions are that every major mature lodgepole pine forest in Colorado will be dead within three to five years.[2]

Roughly 8 million acres, millions upon millions of trees are already dead, kindling for a massive forest fire that will mark their graves. The largest bark beetle outbreak in history is also sweeping across British Columbia, and infestations of similar magnitude can be found in Idaho, Washington, Montana, and Utah. Researchers say an outbreak of this magnitude is unprecedented and that controlling the outbreak is near impossible.[3]

Many Forest Service researchers are convinced climate change is to blame for the monumental beetle infestation. A simple average temperature increase of two degrees is enough to help the mountain pine beetle, normally weakened by frigid weather, survive the winter season with enough vigor to devastate entire pine stands.[4]

Just two degrees is all it takes. Climate studies across the west suggest that indeed things are heating up and winters are, on average, 1.7 degrees warmer. This estimate from the Rocky Mountain Climate Organization and the National Oceanic and Atmospheric Administration may sound like a small increase, but it offers convincing proof that climate change is a reality. These seemingly benign little degrees are likely responsible for the magnitude of the beetle infestation and the current drought along the Colorado River

Basin.[5] Climate change is a reality, not just the talk of ecologists and brilliant scientists. It is our reality.

Turns out my life is directly affected after all.

We gave my oldest son his middle name after a lake surrounded by lodgepole pines in Colorado. Before children, my husband and I spent half our summer weekends near this lake. We gave my son this name, hoping that he would someday hike and fish this beautiful place.

Looks like I may have to cross it off his list.

Do Not Exhaust Your Children

Throughout this book you will find a variety of ideas and resources to help you green up your life and combat the realities of climate change and other looming disasters. Do not do them all. You will exhaust yourself and your children. You will miss your one big thing.

Many moms do a great job of wisely selecting the best opportunities for their family. I struggle here. Often I will stumble across a solid idea and sprint home to make all the preparations for implementing it. The next day I meet another fabulous idea and rush home to set it into motion as well. Of course the project from the previous day still sits unfinished in my mind or on my kitchen table. The result is that my frenetic optimism accidentally hijacks any progress my children made toward understanding just one simple aspect of a planet-friendly life.

In Ephesians 6 Paul offers a few thoughts for family harmony by telling parents not to exhaust their children. This is good advice when faced with a myriad of issues, organizations, and causes. Since there are so many places where we damage the earth, the number of starting points is overwhelming. As dedicated moms we can exhaust our children if we try to do everything. Paul's advice is vital.

Do not exhaust your children.

So where do you want to begin?

Green Steps

1. Teach them to love the earth: adopt an animal.

Several conservation organizations as well as local zoos have animal adoption programs. The World Wildlife Fund is a great example (www.worldwildlife.org). Your child can pick from roughly eighty different endangered species and receive an adoption certificate.

Through the Audubon Society (www.audubon.org), your kids can adopt endangered lady bugs, mosquitoes, and, yes, even dung beetles. Adoption through a conservation organization channels valuable funds to securing the habitat and health of the animals your children choose.

Adoption closer to home, through your local zoo, provides the opportunity to visit the animal. Most zoo adoptions come with regular updates, newsletters, or activities for children to do both at home and on visits. If you adopt through an out-of-town zoo (for example, see www.sandiegozoo.org), you can make visiting your animal part of a vacation experience for your family.

2. Track an animal or habitat.

If donating money to save an animal is not the direction for you, simply tracking the life of a local animal or habitat area offers another way to learn. Finding local forest preserves and open space campaigns in your community, or simply tracking an animal at your zoo are ways to gain some free green ground. When our local zoo boasted the arrival of a baby dolphin, we had our noses pressed up to the tank the day that baby made her public debut. Three months later we visited again, and my preschooler marveled at her size and ability to "swim so good for a baby fish."

If not animals, then track the progress of preserved wetlands, prairies, newly planted stands of trees, or whatever gets your kids into the process of preservation.

3. Help them discover their one big thing.

The examen process highlighted in the first chapter is one way to discover what your child's one big thing will be (as well as your own). This consistent opportunity to talk with your son or daughter provides a glimpse into what he or she is passionate about. Does he keep bringing up the beach or whales? Is she obsessed with camping out or starry skies? Of course kids can be enthusiastic about just about anything, but moms know that some excitement sticks for good. The possibilities connected to this endless energy and fascination might point you toward their one big thing. Here are a few ideas to nudge them along:

Take your overactive ones hiking. Help them learn trail maintenance by clearing small sticks and debris out of the way. Check out the American Hiking Society (AHS) website for organized trail events in your area (www.americanhiking.org). Many are family friendly and a wonderful way to burn energy and spend a day together. The AHS also sponsors National Trails Day, a nationwide event where local hiking clubs and organizations host events that celebrate our 200,000+ miles of national trails in the US.

Take your bookworm to the library to grab books on helping kids save the earth. The following are resources filled with activities for children:

Nature in a Nutshell for Kids: Over 100 Activities You Can Do in Ten Minutes or Less by Jean Potter (Hoboken, N.J.: John Wiley & Sons, 1995).

I Love Dirt: Fifty-Two Activities to Help You and Your Kids Discover the Wonders of Nature by Jennifer Ward (Boston: Trumpeter Books, 2008).

Teaching Kids to Love the Earth: Sharing a Sense of Wonder ... 186 Outdoor Activities for Parents and Other Teachers by Marina Lachecki (Minneapolis, Minn.: University of Minnesota, 1991).

Take your mini-engineer or architect on a tour of your house. Help her see how many lights and appliances are on at any one time. If she is old enough, have her keep an appliance log. How many lights are in use and for how long? Time the washer and dryer: How long are the cycles? Is there a way to shorten them?

Dub this child the energy enforcer and have her make sure no one commits an energy crime (running the dishwasher only half full or the dryer for just one shirt). Her one big thing might be reducing carbon emissions, and she might also be your best advocate for your energy bill!

You can do the same thing with water use. Time showers and dish washing, and be sure family members turn off faucets when brushing teeth. Do you really need to water the lawn? Have this child decide and then keep track of the water use.

Make a Nature Book — my friend Liz put to use one of the many photo albums she received when her son was born. When they go for walks they collect sticks, leaves, and whatever else looks interesting to her son or daughter. They place them in the photo sleeves, and when they get home they look these items up and discover what they are. You can help younger kids fall in love with God's creation by helping them define and learn what is around them every day.

Is your child competitive? My friends Nia, Michelle, and Liz all comment on how their children are very into recycling. They teach them to look for the arrows and to determine which bin items go into. You can coach your kids into trying to have more recycled items on trash day than actual, headed-for-the-landfill trash. See how small you can get your trash can when compared to your recycling bin or to the neighbors' cans.

Your Eco-Examen for Chapter 2

❑ What is one idea from this chapter you would like to implement? Why?

❑ What is one suggestion you will choose to skip? Why?

Eco-Snobs:
How Much Will This Cost Me?

So what's the deal with organic dry cleaning?
Is it really worth the money?
MY FRIEND AMY

Can implementing the three R's—reduce, recycle, reuse,
save you money? If you only implemented the three R's
in your kitchen, you would save money.
CATHERINE PULSIFER (AUTHOR AND CONTRIBUTOR
TO STRESSLESSCOUNTRY.COM)

When my husband and I lived in Denver, we of course made plans to travel back home for holidays. One of the many times we flew to Chicago as "westerners" I scrutinized the crowd waiting to board the plane. There were a few awkward tourists dangling ski boots from their arms, making their way home after a slope side trip, and then there was the sea of fleece-wearing locals, sporting high-end technical backpacks. They sipped from bulky Lexan water bottles that were often hooked to their pack by a carabiner. Some of them were wearing their hiking boots—to Chicago. Many looked like they were heading to Mount Aconcagua rather than the Prairie State.

With an air of superiority, they drank from their expensive water bottles while reading the required mountaineering biography. I always felt inadequate around this subculture. Still do. Of course I was sporting the expensive fleece, but my bag was generic and not likely to earn any approving glances. Nor did I speak a lick of the proper mountaineering language. It's not just a Colorado thing either. I have a friend who moved out to a mountain town in Washington and told me that she needed to buy lots of fleece and learn how to climb or she would never fit in. Sort of like showing up in California without flip-flops.

While this scene clearly does not apply to everyone, without a doubt there is a sort of eco-superiority that outdoorsy, eco-savvy people can emit. I fear it hinders many others from joining earth-friendly causes. And this perception paired with thousands of dollars in gear and technology can make a greener life seem completely unachievable and unaffordable.

But living a more sustainable life, as fashionable as it is today, has nothing to do with trendy fleece and everything to do with an open mind and heart toward making life work in a more simple, responsible, cost-effective way. The green life is open to all, regardless of current eco-awareness, economic status, or location. Would we expect it to be any different? If God is calling us to a place of stewardship and care for his earth that ultimately brings us more deeply into relationship with him, then it makes sense that an eco-friendly life would be affordable and accessible to everyone. Just as God himself is.

Many families flirting with a more sustainable life worry that it will cost them a fortune in time or money, or that it will require new gadgets and gear. It's hard to tell which green options are worthwhile and which are frivolous expenses or frustrating hassles. So Green Mamas everywhere can take a deep breath; green living is not a campaign against common sense.

As a mom who does her best to work with her family's calendar and budget, you will find that green living actually helps you focus on needs rather than wants. A greener life is more simple, affordable, and honest. Disposable income is a rarity in most families. With a shift in your perceptions and a few tweaks in your current thinking, a greener life can work for your family regardless of your financial situation. In fact, it can improve your financial situation (Nancy Sleeth's book *Go Green, Save Green* is a great example of this).

Rearranging

Green living means rearranging your time and spending habits, not increasing them. Here are a few quick snapshots of what this might look like for your family.

Some grocery chains reward customers who shop with reusable bags. Grocers save money when we use canvas bags, and many return these savings as an incentive to shop in their stores (the EPA estimates that retailers spend 4 billion dollars a year on plastic bags). The average US family will use roughly a thousand plastic bags per year. Simply converting to canvas totes and receiving an incentive of ten cents on just half these bags would save one family fifty bucks in a year. Not a huge savings but enough to offset the fact that, for example, many biodegradable, phosphate-free cleaning products cost slightly more than their not-so-green competitors.

If you bump the thermostat in your house up a few degrees in the summer and down a few degrees in the winter, you will conserve energy as well as save money on your heating and cooling bills (estimates suggest 2–3 percent per degree). One friend keeps her home no warmer than sixty-five degrees during the winter. They wear sweatshirts and slippers and all are toasty in an extra layer of clothes. Switching to low-energy compact fluorescent light bulbs will cut your energy bill. While the bulbs initially cost a bit more, they last significantly longer than conventional bulbs (but be sure to recycle them after use).

Ninety percent of the energy it takes to wash a load of laundry is for heating the water. Simply switching to cold washing gets most clothing just as clean and saves money. And air drying laundry (inside or outside) is always an option to save even more on an energy bill. I grew up hang drying our laundry in the backyard. My sister and I would toss our damp T-shirts onto hangers and hook them over the branches on our giant birch tree. Of course this meant our neighborhood friends knew exactly what they wanted to borrow from our closets, but it worked marvelously.

My sister-in-law Lisa saves on her water bill by turning off the tap when they brush their teeth, using the same sippy cup all day long, using low-flow shower heads, and washing clothing only when it is dirty rather than after wearing it just once.

There are three quick categories I consider when making green choices for my family. Once I decide which category an option fits into, I am able to determine the financial, ecological, and social benefits before ultimately determining whether to pursue it.

First are the options that invite us to conserve resources like water and electricity. These typically add money to the budget, as monitoring your family's use immediately begins to trim your bills and conserve resources.

Second are options that replace food choices, cleaning, and personal care routines that use products chock-full of chemicals, or originating from a company with shabby environmental policies, with more earth-friendly options (detergents, household cleaners, skin care items, groceries, etc.). Products with integrity may cost slightly more than nongreen versions, but you get what you pay for here.

Choosing to make your own home remedies, grow your own food, or create your own cleaning supplies is ultimately the cheapest way to be green, but it takes time. My friend Kelly does her best to landscape only with native species that need less water and care than varieties imported from another climate. It cuts on water and energy use to care for them, but she had to commit the time to learning what grows best where she lives. I spend many, many hours in the spring preparing my garden. Time is a necessary commodity here.

At this point you need to determine how much time or money you want to invest in the options that fall into this second category. For many green families, the money saved with household conservation efforts from category one offsets the cost of higher priced eco-friendly decisions from category two. Grocery bills or your investment of time might go up, but energy and water bills definitely go down.

Third are options where a direct financial benefit may not instantly pop out at you. At first glance participating in a campaign to build more bike trails in my community does not directly influence our family budget. It will encourage more people to bicycle rather than drive, and this cause I can surely get behind, but a direct financial benefit for my family is not immediately obvious.

However, I saw deeper into the financial payoff of efforts like this when my daughter developed a cough at around six months of age. It was a deep, guttural cough, one that shook her entire body, causing every mom we passed at the park to shoo her children away in fear of croup. It sounded dreadful. Our pediatrician said it might be asthma.

In 2005, 22.2 million people had been diagnosed with asthma.[1] The prevalence of asthma has been increasing steadily since the 1980s. Since 1980, as a nation we have seen a 75 percent increase in asthma cases. Among children birth through age four the increase has been 160 percent.[2]

As with rises in skin cancer, many medical professionals suspect climate change plays a role in these statistics. Higher carbon emissions from more cars on the road and greater energy use in our homes and industries means more pollution is pumped into the developing lungs of our children. So while the immediate financial benefits of a new bike trail in our town are not abundantly clear, a smaller number of cars on the road may reduce instances of childhood asthma, which means fewer doctor bills for our families, and, most importantly, a healthier, inhaler-free life for our children.

If you look deeply enough into the issues, you will find that most conservation efforts benefit the budget as well as enhance the health and well-being of our children.

Balancing Act

How does a wise mom balance the green budget? Like so many things in life and especially in parenting, success begins with a shift in mind-set. My oldest son proudly wears the picky eater badge. For the entire third year of his life, the menu of items he would even consider consisted of fewer than ten foods.

On the days we gambled on a new dish, there was no limit to the amount of cheering, cooing, and woo-hooing that my husband and I would employ, even to introduce something as kid friendly as chicken nuggets. We wanted so desperately to change his mind-set from one that considered food an enemy to one that dared to eat that nugget.

Sensing that the hubbub in the kitchen meant a grand adventure awaited him, my son would on occasion entertain the idea of eating the fine kid cuisine I placed before him, albeit with great skepticism. However, on the days when life did not afford me any extra energy to be the cheerleading chef, I would blandly slap a plate on the table and insist he try it all. These meals always ended with both of us crying. It was all about the mind-set.

A sustainable mind-set will help get the family budget in line with a greener life. Whenever you remember that your ecological efforts serve a greater purpose than simply following the latest trend, even when they require more of your time and resources than you may be comfortable giving, you make a difference.

God's design for our lives includes stewardship of everything we have received. Most followers of Jesus give of their finances and volunteer their time, but stewardship also means responsible living with our cars, homes, energy consumption, water use, and so on. In these areas God provides an opportunity for wisdom and discernment on our part. At the very beginning of Scripture, in Genesis 1, God outlines a partnership that is wider and greener than many of us realize. It is inconsistent if we slap our 10 percent into the collection plate and then head home in a gas-guzzling car and flip on all the lights.

Environmental stewardship is hard. I do not want to skip the luxury of a long hot shower, especially in February, and hauling my old computer and cell phones off to the proper electronics recycling center is a complete inconvenience, especially when it adds one more thing to my Mommy Do List for the day. I would rather secretly bury them in my curbside trash and get on with my life. And spending a few bucks more for the biodegradable laundry soap irritates me (but not my skin or the local wildlife). We may have to make adjustments to our spending habits and use of time, but the payoffs are eternal.

Now, think for just one moment of the summer camps across the world. Those rugged outposts where kids show up to make beaded lanyards and experience nature are avenues where God breathes into the lives of our children. When we curb our consumption and shift what we do spend in money and time to products and efforts that preserve these pristine rivers, lakes, and campfire circles, we ensure that our children and those who follow will have the opportunity to meet with God in these same sacred spaces. Adjusting our spending habits to accommodate a greener lifestyle allows us the privilege of partnering with God as he reveals his magnificence through his creation.

I Feel the Tension

My family lives in a modest suburban community. I serve part-time in ministry and full-time at home. Church work is not known for fat paychecks, so we basically live on one income. Jetting off to the Bahamas or owning a condo in a ski town is not a reality we experience. And in a shaky economy with a husband who works in what is left of the American manufacturing industry, like most people, we are not exactly in a place to haphazardly toss money around. Yet in all the stretching we do to make life work, I have found that greener living opens up some space in our budget. Try a greener journey and you will likely discover the same thing.

I will confess that I wince when paying for organic produce and almost vomit at the cost of properly harvested salmon. I've dreamt of a celebrity lifestyle that boasts a personal chef who dotes on my every earth-friendly culinary wish. Most of the time I am convinced that we cannot eke out another penny to support green causes or buy organic produce, but when I rethink how we spend our money, I find that there are always ways to support the things that matter to God and to my family.

When I began fully pursuing a greener life, grocery shopping took twice as long. I became fanatical about reading labels. For example, some green cleaning products come in smaller bottles but are highly concentrated, so I had to whip out my dusty math skills to figure out number of uses and cost per use. I was desperate to know whether organic foods really were better, so I would sneak out for the occasional thrill of an evening alone in the grocery store reading labels. Anything for some space, I suppose.

And while, overall, an environmentally sound life, taken comprehensively, is actually cheaper to live, I will not lie to you and say that I figured out a way to make earth-friendly grocery bills lower. Unless you are able to grow, preserve, and can all your own food on a quarter-acre slice of the suburbs. In many cases the price tag for organic/fair-trade food and green products is simply higher, but the payoff ecologically and socially is also higher, much higher. In the end this seems like a great bargain to me, the sort of bargain that matters to God. The sort I am willing to sacrifice for.

Beyond their recyclable packaging, many eco-friendly products are born from companies with integrity. They pay their employees fair wages; justice matters to God. Their corporate policies are aimed at enhancing the planet rather than finding the deepest hole in which to hide waste; honesty matters to God. And these companies care about leaving our children a healthy planet rather than coaching them to consume; families matter to God.

The benefits of thoughtful, earth-friendly consumption for our children are vast. We will get to this in chapter 5, but let's just say that the year we greened our cleaning, my oldest son's seasonal allergies almost disappeared. My middle son's eczema outbreaks slowed to a manageable pace. And I slept better knowing their bed sheets and pajamas were no longer washed with toxins.

Green cleaning products may have initially cost us more, but they paid back dividends the same or greater than their price tag. Our medicine cabinet is nearly void of allergy medicine and hydrocortisone, so we've made up the difference. My mind-set shifted to one of stewardship. I've rearranged my budget and know that each purchase makes an impact far greater than the dent in my debit column.

Green Steps

1. Conserving Water and Energy

Conserving water can add a significant savings to your wallet. Here are a few ways to trim your family's water use:

Shorten your showers and consider installing a low-flow shower head. Get a stopwatch for your bathroom and have your kids compete for the shortest shower.

Turn the water off when brushing your teeth. This can save the average American family a thousand gallons of water per year.

Fix that leaky faucet. How much water does it waste each day? Go to the US Geological Survey website and check out their Drip Accumulator (http://ga.water.usgs.gov/edu/sc4.html). Here, you can type in the number of leaky faucets in your home as well as the number of drips per minute, and it will tell you how many gallons of water you lose in a day. This is a great counting and adding game for your kids.

Never run your dishwasher or washing machine unless it is full.

Use native species when gardening or planning a landscape. Native plants do not need the water and care non-native species might require. This is also a wonderful way to teach kids about plant names and your native habitat.

Check out www.wateruseitwisely.com for one hundred water saving tips. Tips are sorted by region so you can find the best water-saving techniques for your area.

Here are a few ways to save on household gas and electric bills.

Look for the government-backed Energy Star label when considering new appliances. This joint program between the Environmental Protection Agency and the US Department of Energy carries some baggage, but it was designed to encourage consumers to purchase products that reduce energy use and greenhouse gas emissions, and this is a good first step. However, we still need to be educated consumers. Some products bearing the Energy Star logo barely make the cut, so read up before buying (www.energystar.gov).

Turn off the lights! Make it a game. Create a tally sheet for each member of your family. If someone is caught leaving a light on, give him or her a mark on the chart. At the end of each week the person with the most marks does whichever absurd task the rest of the family decides. Anything from singing a silly song to making the family smoothies might work. My father-in-law used to charge my husband and his sisters a quarter every time he caught them leaving a light on.

Consider your curtains. Use your windows for more than just peering outside. Opening blinds and curtains on cooler days allows sunlight to heat up your rooms naturally. Pulling down shades on hot afternoons prevents direct sunlight from adding unwanted heat to your home. If you need to replace window treatments in your home, be sure to purchase energy efficient treatments that block heat or cold from invading your space.

Decide what you want to eat before opening up the fridge; do not waste energy gawking at the yogurt flavors with the door open. Also, consider storing your food in glass containers; glass holds its temperature better than plastic. Your fridge will be more energy efficient if you store in glass. My sister-in-law Lisa's fridge advice is to put refrigerated items back immediately after using them. Don't leave the gallon of milk on the table while you eat your cereal because it warms up and your fridge works harder to cool it back down.

Swap out your light bulbs for compact fluorescent light bulbs (CFLs). They will burn longer and lower your electricity bill. Just be sure to recycle them once they wear out or break. They contain small amounts of mercury that, when exposed, are harmful to human health and to the earth. Local options for recycling them vary from place to place. Many hardware stores, home improvement stores, and even local camera stores take them to be recycled. To find a place near you visit www.earth911.org. Also, if a CFL breaks, you need to be sure that you clean it up properly to keep you and your family safe. For complete information on the benefits, precautions, and management of CFLs, go to www.energystar.gov, type in CFL and all the information you need will be there.

2. Be a chic bag lady. Use the Reusable.

After you ditch your plastic bags, if you want a reusable bag with some panache as well as an impact even after it wears out, check out the ChicoBag (www.chicobag.com). This shrinks down small enough to fit into your diaper bag and even into a modest-sized purse. Company founder Andy Keller believes that people would be more likely to use their bags if they could just remember them. His solution was this product that shrinks down to roughly the size of your fist.[3] ChicoBags can also serve as fundraisers for schools and churches; they can be printed with your logo.

And it gets better: a tattered ChicoBag that needs to be retired can be sent back to the company, where it is mailed off to Grateful Threads, a nonprofit that turns old ChicoBags into rugs woven by women who are victims of domestic violence.

Also check out www.ecobags.com. They offer a variety of organic reusable bags beyond the simple canvas tote. You can find string bags (great for taking produce home), woven bags, and a variety of ways to haul your apples home in an earth-friendly way.

3. Banish harmful products from your home.

Check the book *Green This!* by Deirdre Imus out of your local library. The founder of the Deirdre Imus Environmental Center for Pediatric Oncology, Imus believes the recent increases in pediatric cancers are largely due to the poor environmental qualities of our homes. This book is dedicated to helping families clean their homes with safe products. Beware, this one can be an overwhelming eye opener. Imus tells you how everything from VOCs (Volatile Organic Compounds) in carpet to formaldehyde in wood flooring can harm your health.

Watch the fumes. Your dishwasher emits a cloud of soap-laced vapor into your house. For some odd reason my boys are fascinated by our dishwasher vent and stand in the kitchen staring at it, all the while it is pumping soapy fumes into their lungs. Lovely. So I find dishwasher detergents with as few harmful chemicals as possible. We use Seventh Generation Free and Clear Automatic Dishwasher Powder (www.seventhgeneration.com). Sun and Earth also makes a nontoxic line of dishwashing products based largely on coconut and orange oils (www.sunandearth.com). You can also protect your family by making sure you operate your dishwasher when no one is home. Also consider skipping the high heat drying cycle; it uses extra energy that you can save by simply cracking the door and letting the dishes air dry.

4. Walk or carpool whenever possible.

Outside your home you can save big money on gas if you carpool, walk, or bicycle to various places. Now I will admit that for many moms this is easier said than done. I have three children. I cannot haul them all to gymnastics on my bike. Walking to town, which we do often, can be a nightmare for us. My boys are often racing across the neighbors' lawns before we have left our block. At times it is considerably easier for everyone if we just jump into the car to hit the pool. However, if I can carpool I do. Admittedly, even this is tough. Who has the extra room for one mom and three kids, not to mention the three car seats and a double stroller? Carpooling is an eco-accommodation many moms cannot make. If you can, go for it! And if God smiles on you one evening and all your squirmy kids sit still in their stroller, then hallelujah, you can walk to your ATM!

If you choose not to own a car (a good choice) but need wheels, consider a car sharing option like Zipcar (www.zipcar.com), or find local options near you by logging on to www.carsharing.net.

Your Eco-Examen for Chapter 3

❑ What is one idea from this chapter that I would like to try?

❑ What is one idea from this chapter I will not try?

Too Much Stuff:
Curbing Our Consumption

It is wrong to assume that men
of immense wealth are always happy.
JOHN D. ROCKEFELLER

"Do not store up for yourselves treasures on earth,
where moth and rust destroy,
and where thieves break in and steal."
JESUS, MATTHEW 6:19

Lying in my OB's office with a full bladder, flanked by an ultrasound machine and my husband, I watched as the technician moved her probe across my stomach. She squinted, clicked computer keys with that acrylic nail sound only ultrasound techs and travel agents can produce, squinted again, and then moved on.

So far so good, but was it a boy or a girl?

I'd been waiting twenty weeks for this. After two boys and a house filled with semi-trucks and sweat, my heart fluttered at the thought of pony tails and Mary Janes. So when my OB suggested we add a few princess costumes to our toy closet, I immediately began doting on my daughter. There were bloomers and bonnets to buy, sandals for summertime, and she had to have a pile of dresses for Sunday mornings (those babies in the church nursery can be rather discriminating).

She would need bows, leggings, and eventually, of course, a prom dress. Within weeks of our ultrasound, her room was heaving with ribbons, shoes, and a pile of those elastic headbands that I never managed to correctly fit onto her head.

A few months after she arrived, I was jamming laundry into an already overstuffed dresser. Eventually, shutting the drawer proved futile. So I opened the closet, looking for space to stash a collared shirt, only to find every hanger already draped in finery. She also happened to have bins of hand-me-down clothing tucked away in the attic. Did one three-month-old baby utterly incapable of appreciating her fine accoutrements really need all this stuff?

We sponsor several children in impoverished areas of the world, and that same laundry-laden afternoon, an update on one of our children arrived in the mail. The girl we sponsor in Columbia had scribbled a Spanish note in crayon. The caption under her letter read "Jesus loves you." Her teacher also stapled to the letter a picture of this eight-year-old, with wide eyes, a wary smile, and a shabby black jumper staring at us from 2,700 miles away. She was dusty and barefoot.

Apparently mothers in her village did not frequent Stride Rite.

She did not have a bedroom filled with outfits for every season, and she did not spend afternoons at every art and dance class her parents could afford. But deep in her poverty, she knew she was loved by Jesus. She did not need a new pair of jeans to know it. So why did I have so much stuff? Why did I feel more like I was drowning in this stuff than being loved by Jesus? And why was I more concerned with giving my daughter a bloated wardrobe than in providing her with a healthy future?

(Not So) Green with Envy

Our possessions have a traumatic effect on our planet that ripples out in every direction. Almost every purchase, from lawnmowers to lip balm, has implications that can be felt in another ecosystem, state, or nation. Take for example, a seemingly simple pair of jeans. Pesticide-doused cotton, blue chemical dyes, and metal for rivets and zippers are just the beginning of their ecological price tag.

Money is spent on marketing and advertising to convince us these pants fit so perfectly we will feel like our former adolescent selves as we wear them. Shipping companies burn fuel transporting the denim across the ocean and across the country before a mildly interested store clerk will fold and stack them.

To finally pay for them means computers are needed to scan price tags and remove plastic security features. Then of course we need the ever-present plastic bag to tote them home, where we'll wash them in gallons of water only to find they've shrunk and no longer fit quite the way we'd hoped they would.

This is the trail of resources for just one pair of generic jeans at the mall. Manufacturing the average pair of jeans means chemicals leach into our rivers, waste travels to our landfills, pollution pours into our air, and people suffer unfair, underpaid, and sometimes cruel working conditions so that we feel like we scored a good deal. *Thoughtfully tailoring what we consume and why is perhaps the single most important green move that we can make for our families!*

If we all engaged in a bit of green discernment before making a purchase, we could make a significant local and global change. By simply deciding not to shop, or at least to shop with integrity when we need to make a purchase, we can give the planet a tremendous green boost. But beware, monitoring your consumption may rank as one of the most unsettling exercises for you and your family.

Without a doubt, this has been the most difficult green move for me.

Let's explore why.

The American Dream

"Life, liberty, and the pursuit of happiness" is the patriotic motto every elementary school student learns with pride. These life-giving words have propelled our nation through many an incident, and while this declaration brings great hope and energy to millions of people, our often mindless pursuit of this American happiness comes with a hefty global price tag.

We consume at an obscene pace. As Americans, we set out to create an idyllic life for our families. We want award-winning schools, chummy neighbors, and lovely homes; so we cram our lives with all the stuff we think it takes to capture these elusive commodities.

We zip off to the kitchen specialty store for the latest cooking gadget to wield at that upcoming dinner party. Holidays increasingly morph into months of shopping rather than moments of meditation and togetherness. We try to impress with clothing, baby gear, vacations, and perhaps even the fact that we worship at the big new church down the street, the one with the ten ga-gillion dollar expansion.

In the process of trying to fashion our lives exactly the way we dreamed they would be, we end up exporting the archetype of the American Dream all over the world. Ours is a dream that implies if people just work hard enough and shop long enough, happiness will be handed over from the drive-thru window. It is a dream that says we can have it all and we would be fools not to take it all.

As Americans sign up for their own version of the dream, much of the rest of the world literally buys in too. To reproduce our utopia, people all over the planet set about consuming at an alarming pace, all to replicate our over-glorified and idealized lifestyles.

How Much Do We Really Consume?

We spend roughly $907 billion per year on discretionary items like apparel, electronics, furniture, and entertainment. Which, according to *Forbes*, is roughly the equivalent of the gross domestic product of Australia (the fourteenth richest country in the world). Then we pour $57 billion per year into the garbage industry to haul it all away when we get bored.[1]

The US consumes about 25 percent of the world's resources yet makes up less than 5 percent of the population. Together, China, India, and the US compose slightly less than one-third of the world's population but are on track to consume more than half the world's resources by midcentury.[2]

So each day freighters filled with trinkets, Styrofoam, steel, paper, produce, wood, electronics, cardboard, chemicals, and, of course, oil arrive at US ports. Each twenty-foot, forty-thousand-pound container is brimming with someone's adaptation of the American Dream.

From the containers to our television sets, our families experience an onslaught of advertising each day, because once that shipment arrives, marketers must convince us we need this stuff. The exact number of ads we are exposed to daily is widely debated (estimates range anywhere from 200 to 3,000 per day). But from buses to bathroom stalls, it seems that every available space our eyes might rest upon has been captured for advertising.

Our children learn a myth at an early age: it is best to consume. This culture of clamoring for more infiltrates the malleable minds of our children. According to the Center for a New American Dream:

Over the past two decades, the degree to which marketers have scaled up efforts to reach children is staggering. In 1983, they spent $100 million on television advertising to kids. Today, they pour roughly 150 times that amount into a variety of mediums that seek to infiltrate every corner of children's worlds.[3]

Marketing to children is big business. Of a mom's discretionary income that she spends on her children, most is spent on apparel and entertainment. So daily you are drafted into the frantic war market-research and advertising companies are in to win your discretionary dollars with their snappy clothes and video games.

Since most families have closets filled with clothes and enough toys to keep their offspring busy for several years, it appears the mar-keting strategies work. I do not need but desperately want these items for my kids. So I load them all in the stroller, and we waltz through the mall looking, coveting, and eventually buying (even when the budget dictates otherwise). And even if we manage to tailor our own consumption, it is often interpreted as offensive should we try to moderate the gifts others give to our children. I have friends who have received everything from giant drum sets and ride-on trains that take up half their living space to kitchen sets that rival their own real kitchen. Generous neighbors can overgive, doting grandparents can overindulge, and well-meaning friends can overestimate the joy that all this stuff brings to our children. Managing the amount of stuff we have might also mean having a few hard conversations about gift giving.

I Want It All

A major electronics chain ran a commercial one winter that has stayed on my mind. A middle-aged man is standing wide-eyed in a big-box store surrounded by televisions offering every size, shape, and color of high-definition bliss. He grins deliriously in a sort of shopping-induced trance, and as he stares into one oversized TV with awe and a sense of arrival, the song "I Want It All" by Queen begins thumping in the background.

Despite my best attempts to avoid our consumer culture, I get caught up in the hype. I want it all, and I want it now.

We're on our way to the park when a bus with a billboard whizzes past and suddenly I find myself dreaming of new suede boots for winter. The whole time I am on the playground I may mentally rework the budget as well as the remainder of our afternoon in an attempt to get a pair of these boots.

I'm also quite content with my sons' room until the Pottery Barn Kids email pops into my inbox. My car seems just fine until I drive past the dealership. I want it all. I want to keep up with the Joneses as well as the Millers, the Smiths, the Coopers, and everyone else in my community. I don't want my kid to be the one with faded clothes or a tattered soccer ball, and I want to be the cool mom with the killer suede boots.

Ask any therapist, pastor, or researcher why we have so much stuff, and you will find a heap of answers. Perhaps we are depressed, bored, overindulged, or making up for some deficiency from our own childhood. Maybe we are anxious and need a diversion from the harsh realities of life, or we never learned the proper perspective on how much is enough.

These suggestions all point to a separation from God our Creator. We were divinely created with all we needed to find fulfillment in this life. God gave us the world, and all we saw was the one thing we could not have, so we plucked that fruit from the tree and have been clamoring for more ever since.

Even with the hope we find in Jesus and the reminder that we will be given all we need (see Matthew 6:28–34), we still do not live like we believe his way is best. He warns us not to store up for ourselves earthly treasures that will rot away, but I pile up my goodies like a squirrel heading into winter.

Theologian Miroslav Volf suggests that we live in a culture that sets us up to buy and sell, not to give and receive. We are not overtly calculating and cruel in our every maneuver, but Volf believes that we move through this life subtly, and often subconsciously, using any edge we might have to gain that proverbial upper hand. It may be money, education, sex, political connections, personality, charm, or any other tool that gives us power over others.[4] We are under a false illusion that this power somehow brings us closer to our dreams. That the upper hand in everything from real estate to Little League moves us closer to our desires for success and happiness. If we are not careful, we might unknowingly make our relationships about what we can get rather than what we can freely give. Jesus taught the opposite. In his simple words, "it is more blessed to give than to receive" (Acts 20:35).

I should be content knowing that my heart is filled with a generous love from God that will satisfy my soul if I let it.

This should be enough. But I still want it all.

In the US, a family of four who lives on less than $21,000 a year is considered to be living below the poverty level.[5] This income level is higher than what 89 percent of the world earns (check out www.globalrichlist.com for a witty little glimpse at income levels across the world). This is not to belittle or downplay the rigors of poverty in the US, but in the middle of their fight for dignity and resources, those struggling in the US can visit a food pantry, seek government aid, or enroll in a variety of community and nonprofit programs.

In parts of the world ravaged by famine, there are no food pantries, just bloated stomachs. Where disease reigns supreme, people walk miles each day for AIDS and malaria medication. Where there is war, corruption robs deserving citizens of international relief meant for them. There is no respite from the suffering, not even a hot meal and a shabby bed in a shelter. It is rare that someone dies of starvation in the US. It is an hourly event across many parts of the world. In fact, according to the UN Food and Agriculture Organization, 6 million children die each year of hunger-related illnesses before their fifth birthday.[6] Most of these children do not live in the US.

When I am able to put my life into this sort of perspective, it helps curb my appetite for more. Sure my neighbor has better decor and a newer car, but, overall, I can still throw away more food in one week than some families eat. So we are doing more than okay.

The Real Price Tag

The impact of our consumer-driven culture that never seems satisfied reaches into every green corner of our lives. Because snappy packaging is more likely to attract a buyer, truckloads of unnecessary plastic, cardboard, and other packaging ends up in our landfills. Some estimates suggest that fully one-third of our landfills are packaging. Because we need room for more shopping venues, wetlands are filled in and forests are leveled to make room for the vanilla, neon-lighted strip malls.

Our children grow up comparing themselves to one another and at an early age wonder why some kids have more than they do. My oldest son was barely four when we attended a play date hosted in a lovely, spacious new home. The hardwood floors were flawless, and the couch so comfy I wanted to retreat there all day. The basement held more toys than our preschool. We played there all morning, and it was perfect play-date bliss.

After walking through our back door with the broken handle, the one-level ranch-style home we lived in at the time suddenly seemed so dingy. Maybe it was cloudy that day. Maybe I was just jealous. My son trailed off to his room as I unpacked the car. When I came inside, he was standing like a slouch in the middle of our kitchen. He sighed dramatically and told me he would be eager to play again at Eric's house because Eric's house was cleaner and bigger than ours. Then he shuffled off to his bedroom, suddenly bored by all the toys that normally brought him joy. They were so plain compared to Eric's toys. I flopped onto my worn-out couch, and as the springs jabbed me in the tailbone, I exhaled slowly and mumbled that I felt the same way.

In just one morning his sharp little mind had already calculated where we were lacking.

Which is ironic because our toy closet was so packed you could not close the door.

We often look toward what we do not have rather than looking right in front of us at all the luxuries we can celebrate. The realities are that we throw away more each year than most people throughout history have ever owned. A friend once confessed to tossing out a thirty-three-gallon trash bag filled with wearable shoes and clothing. Rather than suffer an inconvenient trip to a thrift store, she tossed them to the curb and, adios, off to rot in the landfill for five hundred years.

The average American throws away sixty-eight pounds of clothing per year.[7]

Our consumption heaps overwhelming stress on our local ecosystems, as well as those across the world. To fuel our caffeine habit, coffee growers in Columbia clear cut forests. Our demand for petroleum-based products and transportation has each driver adding about six tons of CO_2 to the air each year.[8] To feed our processed food obsession, rain forests in Indonesia are leveled to create palm plantations. Our consumption has a price far greater than the dollar amount on the tag, both spiritually and ecologically.

So when it comes to greening up our lives, you can see now how the biggest changes do indeed come from curbing our consumption. Finding contentment with everything from our homes to a new baby's wardrobe will impact the planet in ways that will ripple across the globe.

Green Steps

1. Find a new dream.

What are the conscious and subconscious motivators for your family? What does your family dream about? This is a big question, but discovering what ultimately motivates the life of your family can be the first step toward monitoring your family's consumption.

Start asking your children what brings them joy. Again, the exa-men process outlined in chapter 1 is a wonderful way to discover what motivates your children. Are they motivated more by relation-ships or by gadgets? What about the rest of the family? Begin taking an inventory of what brings joy as well as stress to your family. Here you will begin to discover what you, as the parent, can do to tweak how your children find true joy in their lives rather than the fleeting happiness of whimsical gadgets.

The Center for the New American Dream is a thoughtful, proac-tive organization offering abundant resources for people hoping to make an impact on our consumer-oriented culture. Visit www.new-dream.org to find a variety of programs and activities for families as you think through what you as a family consume and why. Here are two of my top picks from this organization:

Tips for Parenting in a Commercial Culture is a free pamphlet with information on how to help your children make wise choices as well as how to shield them from the onslaught of consumer-driven mes-sages they receive on a regular basis.

"The Wallet Buddy" is a downloadable resource that you can print and add to your wallet. It is a credit-card-sized insert that asks a few basic questions, hopefully to trigger thoughtful spending. On one side is this reminder: "Every dollar I spend is a statement about the kind of world I want and the quality of life I value." The opposite side offers five questions aimed at making your purchases powerful.

2. Declare a commerce-free day (a sabbath from spending).

Consider setting aside one day where you covenant as a family not to spend any money. At first glance this seems rather simple, but it can be increasingly complex. The first time I tried it, I had already failed by 8:00 a.m.; we live near a toll road, and I spent forty cents on a toll taking the shortcut to work. Sneaky little things like library fines, postage stamps, or juice from the machine at school can prevent us from having a truly commerce-free day. Pick a day of the week and make it a thoughtful challenge for your family. At the end of the day talk through what it was like to go twenty-four hours without making a purchase.

Eventually consider making this a weekly habit for your family. It nicely dovetails with God's plans for the Sabbath, the fourth of the Ten Commandments, and, interestingly, the commandment about which God provides the most detail on how to implement.

3. Seek out clothing swaps for moms.

With kids who seem to grow an inch a week, we moms often swap kids' clothes in the well-worn world of hand-me-downs and rummage sales. These are wonderful ways to save a few bucks and make a greener life for our families. But who says clothing swaps are just for kids?

Consider hosting a clothing swap night for your friends. Each mom would bring four or five items she no longer wears but that are in style and in good condition. With a few refreshments, chatter, and some kid-free browsing time, moms can shop one another's items in the hostess's home. The more women, the more clothing that can be swapped.

Another variation on this event would be to charge a few dollars per item that is swapped. The proceeds can be earmarked for a favorite charity or a local family in need. It's a great way to savvy up your wardrobe while making a difference both ecologically and socially.

Your Eco-Examen for Chapter 4

❑ What is one idea from this chapter I will definitely set in motion?

❑ What is one idea I will do my best to avoid?

Cotton Onesies and Bamboo Sheets:
Eco-Language Lessons

Save the Planet
SLOGAN PRINTED ACROSS A NONORGANIC COTTON T-SHIRT IN A BIG-BOX STORE

Do not use dishonest standards when measuring length,
weight or quantity. Use honest scales and honest weights.
LEVITICUS 19:35–36

The summer before my sophomore year, two friends invited me to join them for a week at a Young Life camp in the mountains. I'd never been to a Young Life meeting and knew nothing about them, but there were several very cute boys going to this camp, so I organized all the appropriate paperwork and nagged my mom until she said yes. Later that June I packed my bags and hopped onto a charter bus for what became one of the most memorable weeks of my life.

Once I arrived, there were all the usual camp shenanigans like bonfires, hiking, and chasing those boys. Every evening, when the chaos of another day had settled, we had a few moments to reflect as all of us campers were corralled into a giant meeting space. There we sat huddled together on the floor, listening to an animated youth leader talk about Jesus for a while. At first I was completely confused and more than a little bit bored, but by the end of the week I started to find this Jesus guy quite compelling.

Eco-Language Lessons

I grew up in an adventurous family. Every Sunday my parents dragged us everywhere from museums to apple orchards, but never to church, so matters of faith were very new to me. All this Jesus talk at camp was a little overwhelming, to say the least. On the last day of the week I decided I would take a step and try to figure all of it out. So I marched myself right over to the camp store and bought my first Bible. I had no clue there were different versions, so I grabbed the one with the navy blue cover (it matched the rugby shirt I was wearing). I was determined to figure out who exactly this Jesus was and what he meant for my life.

This would prove a more complicated journey than I'd been told at camp. I started attending a local youth group where other students talked about things like Sunday school, small groups, and devotional times. I had no clue what these were. This high school ministry was about to send several students out on a mission trip. I did not understand why they were going or what their mission was. Other students used odd words like *redemption, salvation,* and *savior.* I remember daring once to come to a Sunday school class where the teacher pulled two students up front for a competition. They were pitted against one another in a race to see who could list all sixty-six books of the Bible in order, or come as close as possible.

Someone really won.

I still cannot do this. The Minor Prophets trip me up every time.

For my fifteen-year-old self, and for many people, discovering a faith in Jesus means learning a whole new language. I often left that youth group hopeful yet confused as I chewed on a word or phrase that was new. I was a child of the 1980s, and while I had big hair and cable knit sweaters, I did not have access to Google, so learning this new terminology proved a bit challenging. Everything in American culture, from engineering to scrapbooking to green living, has its own vocabulary. Learning to navigate it is essential to joining a conversation about any of these pursuits.

Even with the recent flurry of green activity, it can be difficult to understand what all the eco-mumbling means unless we learn to speak the language. This is one part of the green journey that takes a bit of time. Most moms I know start their days well before 6:30 a.m. There are babies to nurse and toddlers who need fresh diapers. First graders can never find their shoes, and junior high students just roll their eyes at every lunch option you offer. By the time everyone is buckled into his seat and ready to go, you might already find yourself glancing at your watch and counting down the hours until bedtime.

Once you drop them off, you are on your way to the office or the grocery store or the play date, where you find another set of exhausting issues waiting. So when it comes to learning the green lingo, I understand why many moms toss their hands up and surrender. Who has time to determine what exactly *eco-friendly, sustainable, green,* or *organic* really means when three kids are pulling cans off the shelf in the store? Is green living really worth this much effort? Why can't I just grab something that says "natural" and hope for the best?

Natural, Healthy, Earth-Friendly, Inspired by Nature

Because interest in green living has skyrocketed, many companies have discovered that another shade of green can be made by enticing you to buy their products, even if they are not truly planet-friendly. Corporations make deceptive maneuvers when it comes to labeling their goods, from outright lies to vague yet appealing terms employed in selling their items. And since the FDA does not currently regulate the use of terms like *green, natural,* or *earth-friendly,* it is easy to dupe the uneducated consumer. However, once you know the whole story, you can focus your energies on what really makes a difference and skip all the hype.

For example, statements like "made with natural ingredients" or "naturally made" are found on egg cartons, frozen meals, body lotion, and thousands of other products. What do these words really mean? The word *natural* can mean just about anything the company wants it to mean.

Also keep in mind that a shorter shelf life is actually a good thing. The longer an item sits on the shelf the more perservatives are needed to keep it edible. So you, as the consumer, must flip the box over and read the list. What is in it?

A good product will define its terms. Can you pronounce any of the ingredients? Does it contain bleached items, flavor additives like MSG, or unnecessary dyes? If so, it is not so natural. Look for simple products with short ingredient lists that are as close as possible to the way the items are found in nature. Take for example refried beans (we eat a ton of quesadillas at our house). You can find cans that read "ingredients: pinto beans, salt, water." Or you can grab the can right next to it that reads "ingredients: pinto beans, lard, salt, water, artificial flavoring." The first option is the better can of beans.

Unbleached flour, juice jugs filled with 100 percent juice, dye-free medication, and laundry detergent without artificial perfumes are examples of product labels that come closer to backing up a claim like "natural." Looking for the ultimate in natural? Grow your own food in an organic garden or make your own skin care and bath products straight from the plant itself. Want mint in your tea? Grab a leaf from a windowsill plant in your kitchen. Want a fresh-smelling room? Pluck a few lilac flowers from your yard and plop them into a vase.

Greenwashing is the term that many in the earth-friendly conversation use to describe marketing that entices you to believe the planet somehow benefits from your patronage, when really there is either very little or no benefit. Understanding a few terms and taking time for a quick bit of research, can transform overwhelmed moms into smart green shoppers.

Waltz down your grocery aisle, and you may also notice that from diaper packages to liquid soaps, naturally inspired designs line the shelves. Intricate, earthy logos and neutral colored packaging wrap around everything from tofu to tissue boxes. Chlorinated baby wipes can cover their chemical scent with "natural fragrances," and bubble baths might boast a "gentle wash" even when several ingredients are suspected carcinogens like parabens and Titanium Dioxide.

Green Marketing Maneuvers

Savvy green moms can try to avoid deceptive marketing by asking a few questions before making a purchase. Does the product you are about to buy explain to you exactly how it is green, or does it simply look green? Take a closer look at the claims on the package and compare them to the ingredient list on the back. Do they match up? Is the product certified by a reputable organization (an organic food or fair-trade organization)?

Read the ingredient list. How much of the product is made from fillers? Fillers are additives that the food industry uses to keep cost down by bulking up a product. This sounds okay at first, but it means that when you buy meat, you are not just getting meat. Sometimes as much as 30 percent of the product comes from fillers. Often these fillers include chemical and high sodium additives that alter the color or flavor and damage our health. They can also rob us of the real taste of an item. Soy, sodium, maltodextrine, and something called mechanically deboned meat (ground up meat from other animal parts) are routinely added to many of the the foods we eat.[1]

In addition to food additives, the distance our groceries travel makes an impact on our health and the planet. Conservative estimates suggest that our food travels some 1500 miles to land on our kitchen table. According to a study by Iowa State University, the average American meal includes food that has been shipped from five different countries and that the total number of miles our food travels is steadily increasing.[2]

If you add to this the complex ingredient lists we have today, for something as simple as, say, ranch dressing, it is possible that thousands of miles of shipping went into delivering that salad dressing to your table. From the gas you used on your trip to the store to shipping preservatives, dairy products, and spices across the country to the factory that manufactured it. Then add the lettuce from California and carrots from Michigan and you have burned through more than your share of CO_2 for dinner.

Another powerful green marketing maneuver is using the future health of our children to sell products. Take a brief inventory of the "green" commercials you see with children running through an open field, arms outstretched on a sunshiny day. Happy children laughing and playing on an idyllic afternoon can sell everything from fabric softener to SUVs. It is easier to sell people on a green idea when children are involved, but bringing home many of these items ultimately harms the very children who persuaded us to buy them!

Companies offering green goods are gaining a larger share of their respective industries. In 2008 consumers expected to double the money they spent on green products and services, totaling an estimated $500 billion each year.[3] Five hundred billion dollars is a powerful motivator for a company to go green, or at least to look green.

In the past decade, organizations as common to the American life as the NFL have made green claims. According to *USA Today*, many companies like Target, Nike, Dell, Ford, General Motors, Enterprise Rent-a-Car, Coca-Cola, and Bank of America claim to be implementing greener corporate policies.[4]

A widening variety of social and cultural events also boast a few green advances. The Super Bowl and music festivals like Lollapalooza and Bonnaroo have made green strides as athletes and rock stars arrive in buses fueled by biodiesel, purchase carbon offsets, sell organic cotton concert tees, or beef up recycling efforts. Some of these shifts are truly moves toward a greener life, but for many companies a genuine green difference has yet to be seen.

In 2008 even Barbie claimed to have gone green. Just in time for Earth Day, Mattel introduced what it called an eco-friendly line of accessories for girls. Toy manufacturers took the fabric remnants normally discarded after making Barbie and other doll clothing, and turned them into hats and handbags for young girls.

At first glance this is a lovely idea, though hardly enough to call Barbie green.

The reality is that Barbie is produced overseas with enormous amounts of plastic and packaging, most of which is not recycled. Estimates suggest that since Ruth Handler sold her first Barbie in 1959, roughly one billion Barbie dolls have been sold in over 140 countries. The average Barbie aficionado owns eight dolls. So while these patchwork handbags were sewn from materials that would have been discarded, this does not necessarily make Barbie green. Mattel could truly go green by reconsidering how Barbie is manufactured and distributed worldwide, and with what materials she is dressed and packaged.

The Green Washing Index (www.greenwashingindex.com) is a snappy little website that invites consumers to report instances of greenwashing they have picked up on their own. You can consult their site to see if goods and services that you use are listed, or you can post a greenwashing discovery of your own when you stumble across one.

Learning to Read

Reading labels is the first step in filtering through our greenwashed culture. Several years ago I purchased a box of breakfast bars for my son. He's got a thing for strawberry cereal bars. Slapped across the front of the box, in bold type, was the word *organic*. I glanced at the box for a quick second then threw it in the cart claiming victory against artificial chemicals. Done deal, now off to the produce aisle.

After arriving home I read the box more closely. The ingredient list was filled with lovely items like bleached flour and preservatives like BHA and BHT and others whose names I still cannot pronounce. Turns out the front of the box read "made with ORGANIC strawberries."

There was just one organic, earth-friendly ingredient in the entire box. I read the label, albeit a little late. Now I knew what to look for. I wanted to be sure I was truly giving my kids and the planet the healthy options I was paying for. If this is what you want as well, then you need to take a close look at the labels on your products. Most moms I know are already savvy label readers. Words like *high-fructose corn syrup* can give us the shivers. Too much sugar tells us to skip that item, or at least avoid it around bedtime. When it comes to green living, it is imperative that we read the labels to find out how "organic" or "natural" a product really is.

Organic Chemistry

Few words in the green-living dictionary are fraught with more tension than the word *organic*. Hoards of people orient their lives around organic products, while others wince or laugh at the mere suggestion that organic broccoli is better for you. Some consider organic shopping simply a matter of preference, while others consider organic items absolutely vital to their health and our ecosystem (for example, Oregon Tilth estimates that 67 million birds die each year from recommended pesticide use).

I did all I could to avoid chemistry, so when it comes to defining the word *organic*, I realize that the first and clearest definition of this term has already been reserved for scientists much smarter than I. However, as murky as chemistry and biology are to me, the word *organic* becomes even more roily when applied to food and other products. How do we know if we are truly getting an organic product? Who determines that it is organic? And what does organic even mean, anyway?

There is now an organic version of everything from chocolate to cheese sticks, and people are literally eating them up. In 2003 organic food sales in the US were $10.4 billion and since 1990, sales of organic goods have increased 20 percent each year (this is about five times faster than food sales in general). More than half of all Americans have tried at least one organic product.

The quirky little thing here is that organic food is really nothing new. Organic farming is what almost every farmer and rancher did for centuries, before the widespread use of pesticides, GMOs, growth hormones, and shady waste removal strategies infiltrated the American grocery store. This was the era before seventeen-letter words showed up on the back of your soup cans. Before we pumped strawberries full of chemicals and trucked them up from Mexico, hoping they will stay red and "fresh" en route to Detroit in February. Closer to the days when cucumbers went straight from the field down the road to the market and then to your table.

Granola Hippie Guy

One muggy Saturday morning, my friend Jana and I visited a farmer's market in Eastern Iowa. An array of homemade foods set out on folding tables lured us in, and as we searched for a parking place while inhaling the scent of fresh strawberry-rhubarb muffins, we looked at one another and decided that this was undoubtedly the best thing that had ever happened to us.

I had an armload of fresh tomatoes and three loaves of bread after visiting just two stalls. As we continued to browse with coffee in one hand and fresh goodies in the other, we came upon a booth where a pile of bright onesies printed with the word *organic* sat neatly folded in three rows.

The Green Mama in me was instantly giddy.

The guy behind the booth was probably in his early thirties with gritty hair, dirt-stained jeans, and an old T-shirt. He had that granola sort of vibe that made me suspect he slept on a bed of mushroom compost and bathed in patchouli. My fresh jolt of caffeine prompted me to start yammering away. I posed what I initially thought was a rather silly question. I asked him if the onesies that said "organic" were indeed, well, organic.

He paused, smiled an "I was afraid you would ask that" sort of smile, and admitted that in fact they were not made of organic cotton or printed with a safe, soy-based ink; they simply said "organic." I was gnawing on a chunk of peanut butter bread at the moment, so, with crumbs tumbling from my mouth, I stood there speechless. I was shocked, for I naively thought that if someone printed the word *organic* on an item, it would really be organic, especially when sold by a guy who looked as though he walked to the market from Montana.

Had I not considered the origins of those onesies, I would have snatched up the bright yellow one, lugged it home with my tomatoes, and confidently slipped it onto my daughter with misguided eco-joy.

In a culture where green is the new black and earth-friendly options are all the rage, it can be challenging for even the savviest mom to make the best decisions for her family. What is organic, what is good for you?

Putting Tights On an Octopus

I once heard a mom quip that getting her toddler dressed was like putting tights on an octopus. Defining the word *organic* as it applies to food, clothing, and other personal care items is just like this. There always seems to be an arm or a leg still flapping around, not ready to fit into the stockings.

Basically, an organic product is an item grown and manufactured in a way that respects the land, people, and animals that produced it. Organic goods are minimally processed, and the waste generated from manufacturing and farming methods is either reused or disposed of in an earth-friendly manner. Organic products are at least equal to or better than their counterparts when it comes to your health, and they are indeed better for the planet. For example, cotton crops account for 25 percent of pesticide use worldwide. Were those onesies I saw truly organic, my purchase of them (if I truly needed them) would have helped reduce this figure as well as protected my daughter from those chemicals.

So how do you know if you are truly buying an organic item? The USDA currently offers the most widespread certification program in the US, called the National Organic Program (NOP). Sadly, this is a flawed program riddled with ambiguities that give props to large corporations, and it allows definitions to be more lax than many organic farming advocates believe they should be. But the NOP is still valuable to us. It currently offers the only nationwide organic labeling system backed by the US government and is the most visible organic food label available for most consumers today. There are smaller organizations that do a better job than the government here, but they do not have the national visibility and strength of the NOP (www.ams.usda.gov/nop).

The USDA monitors and certifies food products and will allow them to carry the green and white USDA organic label if they comply with federal regulations. Labels are based on the percentage of the product that is organic. Products labeled as "100 percent organic" must be 100 percent organic in their agricultural origins. Products labeled as simply "organic" must contain at least 95 percent organic material. The label "made with organic ingredients" will tell you that at least 70 percent of the material is organic. Anything less than 70 percent cannot receive a USDA organic label.

Do I *have* to purchase organic food? Not always. There are many reasons not to buy organic. For some, it is easier, and often wiser, to shop locally, and you may not have a local organic farmer nearby. For others, growing their own food is the best option. Still others lament the price of many organic products. In this case, pick a few and do the best you can. According to the Environmental Working Group, we can reduce our daily pesticide intake by up to 80 percent by avoiding the fruits and vegetables that most hold on to their pesticide residue (like apples, celery, bell peppers, berries, spinach, kale and other similar leaf greens, and grapes).

What to Pursue

Once you navigate your way through the land mine of labels and product claims, how do you consistently make purchases with integrity? The next step is to consider the company that endorses a particular product or event. Several well-known companies that have served as staples for American families now offer green product lines. This is great news because it puts earth-friendly options within reach of the average consumer, but it also raises serious integrity questions for the company.

Buying these products makes some eco-sense but may not ultimately make the difference we need to change our current ecological trajectory. It is interesting to consider how companies can offer both eco-friendly and traditional products (aka, not so eco-friendly). They may boast that one of their toilet bowl cleaners is safer for the earth than their traditional cleaners. If this is indeed true, then why continue to offer the damaging traditional products at all? Why not convert all product lines to biodegradable and planet friendly if the research proving their effectiveness has been completed and the company is already poised to produce the green products? Why continue to offer both?

As moms, we wield an enormous amount of purchasing power, and wherever possible we should endorse companies with proven ecological integrity from beginning to end. Companies that pay their employees fair wages, recycle their manufacturing and clerical waste, monitor their carbon emissions, and offer ecologically sound products or services make a difference for our children.

The Holistic Approach

This holistic approach to business is honoring to God because God is interested in making our lives whole. Faith can easily become compartmentalized. Many people think of God as interested in just our church attendance, tithing, or fending off of a particularly nasty habit. But God is interested in everything that we do and the big picture of how we live. He wants our bodies healthy and rested, our homes filled with peace, our professional pursuits honest and truthful, our air clean. He is passionate about how we move through every part of every one of our days, not just the Sundays.

When I sit on my couch staring at the television, sipping diet

cola, and eating chocolate chips straight out of the bag, I might wonder why God feels elusive to me in that moment. There are days
when I race from my air conditioned house to my air conditioned car
to the air conditioned store or office and then back again. I hunker
down to avoid any extremes in temperature and end up sheltering
myself from any fresh air. Eventually I find myself wondering why I
feel antsy and agitated. Perhaps it is because I've not spent more than
five minutes outside that day.

Maybe we should try rolling down the windows and taking a
breath of God's fresh air, even on a February morning. Maybe we
should walk to the park instead of driving. Maybe God is calling
to us from the backyard to come outside and play with him; "the
heavens declare the glory of God; the skies proclaim the work of
his hands" (Psalm 19:1). Maybe we need to go outside with our kids,
stretch out on the cool, damp grass, look up, and marvel at the sky
for a bit.

When we find the time to make holistic choices like caring for
our bodies, eating wisely, and breathing deeply the freshest air we
can find, we may discover the fine nuances about God that we have
been missing. When we honor God with our whole lives, we catch a
wider view of his heart for this planet and for our families.

So when we come to the green conversation, if we step back and
look at the philosophy of a company, we can choose ones that honor
these holistic desires of God for our lives. A good friend once told
me this was where she wanted to give up on going green. She was
okay with looking for an organic label, but going the next step and
figuring out which products had integrity was just too much work
for her. It does take time. But once you sniff out the scams and lock
your loyalty into a few solid companies, the green road is wide open,
and getting what you need becomes easier. You've narrowed down
your options and can go straight for the holistic companies you know
work. This saves you time.

It's All Hooked Up

My son once asked me why everything is "hooked up." He then explained how he noticed that the streets were connected to the driveways that were connected to the house and to the car and to the garages and on and on.

He's right, everything is hooked up. My polycarbonate plastic bottle is hooked up to a store that is hooked to a shipping container that is hooked to the dolphins. This is freshman biology. My seafood dinner is directly affected by shark fishing. I do not think of this when I order pasta with white sauce and scallops. Overfishing of hammerhead sharks off the East Coast of the US sends cownose ray populations soaring. The cownose ray eats oysters and scallops. So killing off the big sharks means fewer oysters and scallops for dinner.[5] Plastic grocery bags end up in the stomachs of whales. Heavy water use upstream means drought downstream. Did you know the Colorado River no longer even makes it to the ocean?

Conservationist Gary Nabhan, PhD, states that less than 2 percent of the Colorado River's natural flow actually makes it to the delta and the Sea of Cortez today.[6] This river, the one that happened to carve the Grand Canyon and that rips with vigor across the west is now sucked up to water golf courses and irrigate crops that were never meant to be grown there.

It's all hooked up. If we want to honor the fragile ecosystem we live in, then we need to support organizations, lifestyles, and companies who honor this cycle.

Next time you set out to join a club, support an organization, or simply to buy chicken or glass cleaner, ask yourself if what you are supporting with your dollars cares for people and the planet the way God does. Does it bring people into a better, more holistic, and even more holy way of living? Whether they know it or not, do they envision the kind of world Jesus would encourage? If the answers are yes, then you have found partners that will help you become a greener mama (I'll share a list of some in the next chapter as well as in the appendix).

Green Steps

1. Teach your kids the basics.

Consider downloading the song "Reduce, Reuse, Recycle" by Jack Johnson. You can find it on the *Curious George* movie soundtrack. It is a fun and whimsical way to introduce your kids to a few planet-preserving words.

2. Introduce a word or Scripture of the week.

It always helps to remember that God is the reason we are look-ing for truthful, honest goods and services. So help your kids get eco savvy by pulling a verse about the natural world for them to meditate on each week (try Genesis 8:22; Psalm 148:3; Isaiah 55:12; and Mark 16:15).

Along the way toss in a few other words and phrases that will help them live greener lives. After coaching my oldest son on what recycling meant, whenever I ask him to throw an item away he now asks, "Which trash can, Mom?" He's learned that it matters where the garbage goes, which means he finally learned the word *recycle*.

3. Ask for the Material Safety Data Sheet.

If you are truly interested in discovering exactly what is in a product, you can ask to see the MSDS (Material Safety Data Sheet). Manufacturers do not have to list all their ingredients on a label. However, they legally have to list all ingredients on their MSDS. The MSDS was designed so that medical professionals will know how to treat an individual who has had an adverse reaction to a product. Technically companies must comply and provide you with an MSDS if you request one, but some companies are slippery and will not easily provide this document. Many green companies easily offer this document for all to see. A truly green company should have nothing to hide.

Your Eco-Examen for Chapter 5

☐ What is one idea from this chapter I would like to try with my family? Why?

☐ What is one idea from this chapter I definitely will not do? Why?

Green House:

Making the Changes
That Work for Your Family

Every ordinary moment of ordering take-out bean burritos;
pushing a creaky, metal grocery cart; sorting dirty laundry;
can become a door of vision and hopeful imagination.
JOY SAWYER

This is the day the Lord has made;
let us rejoice and be glad in it.
PSALM 118:24

According to adolescent development experts, families who regularly
eat a meal together seem to manage the drama of adolescence with
a bit more ease than families who skip out on family mealtimes. In
families who eat together at least three times per week, kids seem
less likely to struggle with depression, develop eating disorders,
drink, smoke, or consider suicide.

Doris Christopher, founder and president of the Pampered Chef,
stresses the importance of the family meal (and not just to push her
products). According to Christopher's Columbia University research,
kids who ate fewer than three meals per week with their families,

when interviewed, said they longed to eat together more often. And according to Indiana University research, other than read together, the most important bonding activity that a family can do is share the family meal.[1]

The kitchen table around which these meals are served is a treasured icon for the American family, and the kitchen itself is often the hub of activity. Homework help happens here, and the family calendar or phone hangs on the kitchen wall. The fridge is the object of every hungry or bored family member, and most hosts will agree that no matter how inviting the rest of their home is, everyone gathers in the kitchen for the party.

Around the dinner table we learn about science projects, new friends, hurt feelings, and what everyone likes on her pizza. We manage to stop the flurry of activity for just a moment and give thanks for a meal. We learn to use our napkins, pass the butter, and to quickly sop up spilled milk before it dribbles to the floor.

The table was also central to the life and teachings of early Christians. Jesus knew the importance of gathering around the table and still calls his followers to gather around a meal today. In the book of Luke, we read an account of Jesus appearing to his followers on the road to a town called Emmaus. On this road he walked and talked with them and shared stories with them, but for most of their journey they did not know it was Jesus. Eventually he joined them for dinner. At this meal, with everyone gathered around warm food and stories and conversation wafting through the air, Jesus broke bread and revealed himself to these families.

You can learn some amazing stuff at the dinner table.

Life happens around the table. So when it comes to making the green changes for our own homes, perhaps the best place to start crafting our plan is from the kitchen table.

Starting at the Table

Greening your home by starting at the kitchen table means you begin to implement earth-friendly changes that fit into the center of your family's life. These are changes that fit the natural rhythm of what your family values. So often an idea, green or otherwise, looks fabulous at a friend's house but is a disaster at our house. A sermon idea, green idea, or an idea I gleaned from a magazine fizzles if it does not fit into the rhythm of our family.

This was my experience with cloth diapers. As a mom-to-be, I made a strident vow to keep my baby's bum far away from gel-filled, chemically treated disposables. I knew that my child would go through about five thousand disposable diapers, all of which would end up in a landfill. I knew that collectively, parents send roughly twenty billion diapers to landfills each year. I knew that disposables were chemically treated with chlorine, dyes, and filled with those bizarre little gel balls made from sodium polyacrylate (a substance banned from tampons and considered toxic to pets).

I also understood that my baby would spend roughly 25,000 hours in these chemical- filled conveniences. Their super absorbency would prolong the problem by delaying my potty training efforts. They were designed so my son would not feel wet, so why bother with the toilet?

Plus, I have to admit, I had an air of eco snobbery about me. As I researched cloth companies, I looked down on those hasty moms grabbing disposables off the shelves. I had the nerve to wonder what sort of mother would knowingly cover her precious baby's bottom with disposables, even if they were stamped with Elmo and Winnie the Pooh.

I had the most adorable organic cotton diapers picked out and I would soon be the ultimate eco mom. That was until my son was born and I found myself struggling with a colicky newborn and my own postpartum tears. I was overwhelmed, and the diapers they gave you at the hospital were just so easy. Talk about marketing genius. I caved. Instantly.

This choice continues to gnaw away at my eco-conscience. And for many moms, the diapering issue is front and center in their green conversations. I know moms who are racked with guilt by their disposable choices, and I know cloth moms who feel chided by others and are often told that their cloth decision seems "out there" or almost crazy.

While clearly, sending disposables to the landfill is not helping the planet, diapering with cloth is not exactly a free ride to environmental bliss. I believe it is the better choice and would use cloth if I had it to do over again. But to clean cloth properly, a significant amount of energy goes to heating wash water to temperatures that can properly remove the bacteria (remember, 90 percent of the energy used in a wash cycle comes from heating the water). Should a mom choose to dry them in a dryer, this uses even more energy (my friend uses a brand that suggests she wash them twice each time they are soiled).

Rest assured, this is not the central issue for sustainable parenting! If you are able to make cloth diapers fit into the rhythm of your family, then go for it. If not, use that energy to make wise choices in other areas. Do what you can and lose the guilt over the changes you are unable to pull off at this point in your life.

If disposables work for you, definitely consider chlorine-free diapers and wipes from a company with a sustainable track record. Nature Babycare is my favorite (www.naty.com), and www.tushies .com is another good source. For you cloth gals out there, my cousin Sarah is convinced that Bum Genius is the best (www.bumgenius .com).

One last diaper note: strange as it sounds, the best diaper option may eventually be to recycle disposables — yes, recycle diapers. A company based in the UK called Knowaste (www.knowaste.com) has developed a program to recycle disposable diapers. Pilot programs are running in California.

Eco-Sins

Cloth diapers were a green change that did not work for the rhythm of my family. And if they don't work for yours, you will find no judgment here. Regardless of our shade of green, most of us have some sort of "eco-sin" that we claim we cannot live without. Maybe it is a long shower or plastic baggies for lunch snacks. Maybe you love your gas lawnmower, stand by your hair dye, or crave a favorite snack manufactured without an ounce of eco-awareness.

Greening your life by starting with what works for you will help your family make the choices they can stick with and lose the guilt that comes with the reality that we cannot do it all. Leaving the rest of your green life to sort out another day is perfectly okay, as long as you keep sorting it out. Better to set a few things aside and do them well than slough the whole idea off as impossible.

Your Family's Rhythm

My cool friend Kate gave me a great picture book one Christmas: *The Mommy Book* by Todd Parr. In his book, Parr demonstrates the different ways that moms do life with their kids. Some fly kites and others fly planes, some cook and others order takeout. In his writing is the reminder that each mom has her own rhythm and style of parenting. Honoring this rhythm honors you and your family.

Families with a mom who works at home may implement sustainable practices that are different from a mom who works outside the home. Families who love to cook and celebrate great cuisine may have a different set of green eating habits than a family that orders takeout on a regular basis. For one, organic food, reusable table linens, and nontoxic cookware are important. For the other, restaurants close to home with ecological integrity and minimal packaging are important. You need to know what sort of mommy you are to make the changes that really add up big for the planet. Fretting over cookware you never use will not help much.

The Kitchen Table Exercise

Take a few moments to walk through a day in the life of your family. Start at the kitchen table and move through your house from there. The following is a brief look at activities and habits common to the lives of many American families, with a few ideas on how to green them up. As you move through your home, choose the rooms and changes that make the most sense for your family and begin there. For an interactive resource to help you look at each room in your home, check out *National Geographic*'s Green Guide (www.thegreen guide.com). Under their Home and Garden tab, they offer a guide that takes you through ideas to green up many rooms in your home.

The Kitchen

What does your family eat? Does your house have more produce or more boxes of processed and individually wrapped foods? Do you know where your food comes from and who grew it? One of the best changes we can make is becoming familiar with what we are eating. I talked a bit about organic items in the previous chapter, but eating healthily means taking steps beyond the organic label.

The most sustainable way to eat is by growing your own food. Consider plotting out a starter garden and bringing a few favorite foods to life one summer. If you do not have a yard, you can join a community garden project; most communities have at least one plot offered by the park district or other organization. Even if all you manage to do is dabble in a few herbs that grow on your windowsill, you are cutting down on the fuel and cost of shipping food to the store.

Another way to eat greener is to learn to eat seasonally. Foods that are in season in your region of the world are what you should strive to eat. Where I live I can get a June-bearing strawberry from my garden in the spring, but not in mid-December. So for me to eat seasonally means I skip the strawberries until spring. Seasonal foods are more likely to be grown locally and therefore trucked in from a much closer location, and they are also abundant at local farmers' markets during their harvest time. This means the produce you eat will be fresher and the nutrients they store will be richer, as they will not be lost over time spent traveling. Eating seasonally also means you have a chance to learn what actually grows where you live, what God had planned for the soil in your part of the world. Not a bad little bit of information to have.

In your kitchen you can also consider which paper products you use on a regular basis and consider swapping them for reusable versions. Cloth napkins are a great place to start, and you can make them from scraps of other fabrics you already own. Old table linens no longer up to their Sunday best can be simply cut into squares and hemmed to make napkins. Short on time? Grab a stack at a resale shop; they last for years if you buy a dark color that does not betray your ketchup stains. If you wash them in cold water and hang them to dry, you can save energy on laundering them.

Try making cloth napkins fun for your family. Kids can spice them up with nontoxic fabric paints, they can add their names, or you can decorate them to celebrate a birthday or special event. You might also consider cloth napkins made from 100 percent organic cotton (which means they are free from harmful pesticides and were made with a kind eye toward the environment).

Do you rip through rolls of paper towels? When we began implementing changes for our family I forced myself to stop constantly reaching for them. I was amazed at how the moment a mess appeared my arm went left for the towels. After my babies slurped their way through pureed peas, everything in me wanted to yank off a paper towel, wipe their faces, and then toss the whole oozy mess into the trash.

Instead, I started using damp washcloths to wipe them down. We received gifts of at least four packages of baby washcloths with each child. Since our bathroom was already stocked with towels, I transferred these thin baby washcloths to the kitchen to use instead of paper towels. Microfiber cloths also work great for these jobs.

How do you clean your kitchen? Have you considered biodegradable dish soaps and dishwasher detergents? A biodegradable item is one that can be broken down by living organisms and is normally made from organic material like plant and animal matter, or artificially manufactured material that functions in this way.

When it comes to soaps and dishwashing detergents, a biodegradable product is one that does not pollute or harm streams or clog treatment plants with unnecessary chemical waste, like phosphates. Biodegradable soaps are made from natural ingredients and will re-enter the earth without harming our families or our fragile ecosystems. Check out Seventh Generation (www.seventhgeneration.com), Mrs. Meyers products (www.mrsmeyers.com), or Ecos (www.ecos .com). Most are available at grocery and nationwide chain stores, or can be delivered to your door through the company websites.

The Bedrooms

We spend a significant amount of time in our bedrooms when we sleep. Be sure to open your windows often to encourage natural cross ventilation. The EPA reports that the air inside our homes has two to five times the volatile organic compounds (VOCs) that outdoor air does. These VOCs can come from our cleaning products, paint, waxes, disinfecting materials, markers, adhesives, pesticides, etc. Popping open a window helps clean out your air. Window management is also a great way to cut back on the energy you use to heat or cool your home. Be sure to open or close your windows at certain times of day, and use ceiling fans and window treatments to regulate the temperature before you turn on your AC or heat.

When it comes to the bedrooms, organic and natural fibers for bedding can make a big difference for your family. They can temper tricky allergies, fend off looming respiratory problems, and literally help you sleep better, knowing your snugly munchkins are truly snoozing safely. If you are in the process of creating a new room for one of your children, upgrading from cribs to toddler beds, or buying a new bed for yourself, you may find these green options enticing.

Consider sheets and bedding made from natural fibers. Organic cotton is a wonderful place to start (certified organic is best). You can also buy sheets made from bamboo. Who knew the scratchy-looking trees of every panda poster make for a phenomenally soft night's sleep? Bamboo is the fastest-growing woody plant in the world. It can grow up to three feet per day and provides a resource for fibers that is renewed almost overnight. When sustainably harvested, it creates a solid alternative to other crops that take longer to grow (just a caveat, the recent demand for bamboo has led some manufacturers to clear cut healthy forests to plant bamboo. Whenever possible, read the labels and do your research. Be sure your bamboo products do not harm the very ecosystems we are hoping to protect by using them).

If you are in the market for a new mattress, consider one stuffed with wool or organic cotton. Many traditional crib mattresses are filled with toxic flame retardants like polybrominated diphenyl ethers (PBDEs). Traces of PBDEs have even been found in breast milk. Other mattresses have polyurethane foam that manufacturers use to maintain shape and safety. It is possible to achieve similar goals without sleeping on toxins. Check out Lifekind products (www .lifekind.com) or Naturepedic (www.naturepedic.com) for a few green mattress ideas.

The Bathroom

Most people are open to using paper products made from recycled material for office paper, magazines, and newspapers, but when it comes to personal hygiene items, research suggests the word *recycled* can make folks a bit squeamish. It's fine for the printer, but when it comes to the rear end, many people draw the line.

We cut through millions of acres of virgin forest each year to make simple products like toilet paper and tissue. Since many families value pristine products to wipe their noses and bottoms, a myth that recycled products cannot deliver perfect performance has cropped up. The reality is that if you use recycled products, you and your kiddies can enjoy clean noses and bottoms without damaging the earth.

Buying recycled tissue and toilet papers makes great sense both ecologically and for your family's health (and in case you are wondering, "recycled toilet paper" means toilet paper made from recycled paper, not from used toilet paper!). It is insane to me that we would choose to take care of this messy business at the expense of millions of trees.

If every family in the US swapped out one roll of traditional toilet paper for one roll made from recycled materials, it would save 424,000 trees![2] Eco-friendly papers created from recycled materials use fewer chemicals as well, which means fewer toxins our bodies will encounter. Try it for a week. Pick up a roll of toilet paper made from recycled material and have your family take a test run. It may work for you, and, if so, you have found another simple green maneuver that works for your family. Try Earthfirst, Planet, or Seventh Generation papers.

One last eco-friendly bathroom note: There is a saying that goes, "If it's brown, flush it down. If it's yellow, let it mellow." My California friend Ann taught me this. Each flush of the toilet releases between 1.6 and seven gallons of water. Fewer flushes, fewer gallons down the drain.

Personal Care

The items that come into contact with our bodies on a daily basis are another place where we can see huge benefits to our health, the health of our children, and the health of the planet with just a few simple changes. Our skin, the largest organ of our body, is the daily recipient of toxins from our cosmetics, shampoos, and body lotions. And all the residue from shower gels and soaps that runs down the drain makes an impact on our ecosystems.

The cosmetics industry is notorious for greenwashing and for labeling products in such obscure ways that even the savviest mom can barely understand what she is putting on her face each day. The FDA does not regulate most claims that cosmetics and personal care companies make, so they can label products however they want. I asked my friend Lizzie to help me navigate the world of cosmetics, and after months of research and reading she was still mystified by the labels and all the known carcinogens inside them.

So if you are looking for safe personal care products, or want to see how safe the goods you currently use are, the best place to start is the Environmental Working Group's Skin Deep Cosmetic Safety Database (www.cosmeticsdatabase.com). This nonprofit organization has compiled information on over 42,000 products and will tell you if any of up to fifty toxins have been detected in any one product. Simply visit the site and type in the name of a product, and it will let you know what is truly inside.

The best solutions overall are honestly the ones that come straight from the garden or options that just leave our skin to be as it is. One friend told me that she was going au natural during summer. No make up, lotion, hairspray, hair dye, nada. Just sunscreen (California Baby and Blue Lizard Baby are good ones) and a pony tail holder. Amen to that!

Laundry

What would motherhood be without laundry? First question we've got to ask ourselves when greening up the wash is this: Do we really need to wash it? Block the detergent commercials that boast pristine whites and bold colors out of your mind. Is the shirt even dirty? My kids take a bath at night then put on clean pajamas then hop into a clean bed. So they can surely wear those pajamas all week. Once I stretch out my jeans to accommodate my thighs, I do not, under any circumstances, want to shrink them in the wash. I wear all my pants multiple times. Unless it smells or gets stained, do not wash it.

When we do wash, of course, we need to wash in cold water and hang dry anything we can. Both efforts save on carbon emissions and your energy bill. Using a high efficiency detergent that is phosphate free and biodegradable also makes a big difference to the local ecosystem. Ecos brand is our favorite (www.ecos.com). Charlie's Soap is another good brand (www.charliesoap.com).

If an item becomes stained or damaged beyond wear, reuse it as an art smock or cleaning rag, cut it into napkins, transform the pieces into a patchwork pillow or handbag, or pull the elastic out and make a headband. Try your best to keep it out of the landfill.

Home Improvement

Rebuilding or remodeling a section of your home? First ask yourself if the project is essential, and if so, then consider making your project a green build. As with mattresses, bedding, paper towels, and almost every other household product, there are green and nongreen options for home improvements. The not-so-green options are often laced with chemicals, like pressed woods that off-gas formaldehyde and carpets that emit VOCs. Many are also manufactured with processes that damage the earth, like clear cutting forests, shipping long distances, and treatment with pesticides.

You can reuse resources or seek new sustainable options when it comes to installing carpets and hardwood flooring. There are green options for window treatments, lighting, appliances, and other fixtures in your home. Building a deck? Consider using a product made from recycled plastic. My parents have a deck built from recycled plastic. It looks like wood, but I believe it is far superior. No need to stain it or treat it as the years go by, and my little ones don't get splinters when they race their trucks across the floor. HGTV offers several green decorating tips on their website. Also visit www.getwithgreen.com to find green options for different areas of your home, or look up local green architects and builders in your area through Green America's National Green Pages, a nationwide directory of green businesses and organizations (www.coopamerica.org/pubs/greenpages).

Remove the Barriers and Make It Obvious

My middle son was barely eighteen months when we first attempted to complete a puzzle together. It was nothing fancy, just a fish-bowl-shaped puzzle with three giant sea creature pieces. There were even big knobs for his chubby hands to grasp. As I set the puzzle on the floor, I had the audacity to wonder if this project would be too easy for him. If you've ever worked puzzles with a toddler, you know I was clearly mistaken.

After I repeatedly called my son into our playroom, he finally responded by plopping in front of the puzzle with a train in his hand. I explained to him the intricacies of doing a puzzle while he looked around the room for something a bit more catchy to play with, like my laptop cord. Eventually I ended my discourse and laid the three wooden pieces beside the frame and encouraged him to help the fishies find their homes.

He took the red lobster and jammed it into a nearby plastic dump truck.

Again, I corralled all the pieces, and the second time he snatched the sea turtle and repeatedly tried to slam it into the lobster space. This sort of charade went on for several minutes with no success.

We were both frustrated, so after a quick break for milk and graham crackers, we tried a new approach. I put only one piece immediately in front of him and filled in the other spaces myself. All he had to do was grab the yellow fish, twist it a few times, and voila! I removed all the other options and, finally, victory was ours.

Sometimes, if we remove all the barriers, we can solve the puzzle.

Organizing your home for green living is a bit like solving a puzzle with a toddler. Kids are easily distracted, so giving your family too many choices will only confuse and complicate your green efforts. We have to make it obvious. Remember your One Big Thing from chapter 2? This is the sort of clarity that can make the green life run a bit more smoothly in your home.

Green living at home also means that visitors, friends, and Uncle Larry might be prompted to ask questions about your emerging lifestyle. For example, our boys have flashy stainless steel sippy cups. Yes, stainless steel sippy cups. After researching the wiles of plastic manufacturing and waste, I was convinced that, for the health of my children and our planet, we should try to avoid drinking from plastic.

These cups are flashy, literally, and sometimes they squeak loudly when my kids suck on them. Our noisy, shiny cups have accumulated their fair share of questions from other moms. From "What on earth is that?" to "Hey, that's a cool cup, where can I get one?" (www .kleankanteen.com). Each conversation is an opportunity to share, in a few simple sentences, what I know about plastic and the planet.

It's the same sort of opportunity that I find when a mom asks me why we go to church or where we go to camp. I love to chatter away when someone asks me about these things because I believe they make a difference. Simple encounters like these, whether over sippy cups or bigger things like faith, bring opportunities to share what we know about God's world.

Green Steps

1. *Try one of these simple ways to make it obvious.*
   Put the eco-friendly options your family chooses front and
      center.
   Hide the paper towels and put the reusable options within
      reach.
   Put the recycling bin in a prominent place (it should be bigger
      than your trash can).
   Post little notes and signs to remind everyone to turn off
      lights.
   Buy a water filter and reusable bottles. Remove disposable
      bottles.
   Always put your reusable shopping bags back in your car.
   Hang a clothes line to line dry laundry.
   Put a note on your thermostat that says "Get a sweater." It will
      remind family members prone to bump it up a few degrees
      to layer it up instead.

2. *Replace with purpose.*
   Do not dash out with a green list and swap out half your house for greener options. Most of us cannot afford to do this anyway,

but the very real temptation to rework your entire world is there. Some items can be replaced quickly: food items, containers for eating, swapping out paper for cloth.

But replacing a not-so-green product that still works well with a new green product can still harm the environment! My friend Megan told me about a great broom she saw made from reclaimed material and bamboo. Her sister Meredith pointed out that she already had a broom. "Why do I need that one?" she asked. Good question. If you already have a broom, keep it. To replace items in perfect condition would be a waste of resources. The earth-friendly goods still use water and electricity when they are manufactured, and they guzzle gas and oil en route to your local store. Wait until you honestly need to replace them, and then go for the green. Sometimes the greenest option is finding contentment with what you have.

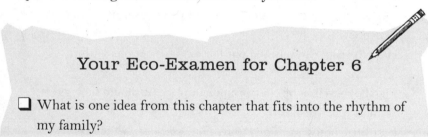

Your Eco-Examen for Chapter 6

❑ What is one idea from this chapter that fits into the rhythm of my family?

❑ What is one idea from this chapter that goes against my family's rhythm?

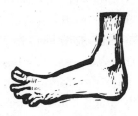

Carbon Footprints:
What's Your Shoe Size?

Only within the moment of time represented
by the present century has one species—man—
acquired significant power to alter the nature of his world.
CONSERVATIONIST RACHEL CARSON

The least movement is of importance to all nature.
The entire ocean is affected by a pebble.
BLAISE PASCAL

One Saturday on a family weekend out of town, I snuck out for a jog down a rural Wisconsin highway. It was a perfect summer morning. Sunshine and cheerful little chipmunk forest noises greeted me as I dashed into a world of skinny pine trees and rustic cabins. I shuffled along, quite satisfied with my current nature fix, until I noticed a strange mechanical murmur grumbling from a nearby stand of trees. At first it sounded so low and growly it was barely noticeable, but it grew louder as I approached.

The noise felt out of place against a backdrop of swaying grass and beams of sunlight threading themselves through the trees. Agitated that my reflective moment was disrupted, I honed in on the noise to discover it came from a hard-working, banged-up turquoise machine, just a few feet off the shoulder of the road.

A pudgy man was sitting inside the cab of this mini-bulldozer-like contraption. He pulled a few levers every now and then but mostly just sat there expressionless. The machine was small. There were two tractor treads for moving and a claw sticking out of the front. It was remarkably quiet, considering what it was. I watched for a moment as the pudgy man with the levers positioned his claw around the trunk of a red pine and then, with an air of efficiency, yanked it down.

The tree trunk surrendered by bending quietly. Sort of like dandelions do when my kids bring them inside. After breaking the trunk, this machine began pulling and chattering along the length of the tree. It chewed off twigs and branches like corn on the cob. Soon it was no longer a tree but a naked log lying next to a pile of pine brush.

It smelled like Christmas.

I was indignant. How could that mean pudgy man with the levers rip down those trees? How did he sleep at night? Didn't he know that the forts and hideouts of a million childhood adventures lay undiscovered in those trees? I declared him my enemy.

As I ran along, fuming with self-righteous anger, I came across rows of trees that were slated to suffer a similar fate; I saw a sign boasting that the land was owned by a paper company. Those trees probably ended up in my printer at home or the copy machine at work. That very moment I realized I was asking the wrong questions. I could not blame this man for doing his job. He needed a paycheck. I wanted paper. Everyone got something out of the deal.

The real question was how could I sleep at night? How could I print off reams of paper or rip through rolls of paper towels without even flinching? How could I keep feeding my insatiable, consumer-driven desires and still blame our ecological disasters on the logging or the paper industry? Maybe I should declare *myself* the enemy.

My life is a total dichotomy.

I simultaneously desire for my children all that is wild and natural, and at the same time I want a pile of toys wrapped up all pretty at Christmas. I print party invitations with piles of virgin paper, but I want all the forests intact when we decide to go camping. What I realized that morning was that before we turn around and blame ecological tragedies on others, we have to point the finger at ourselves.

Jesus said it best in Matthew 7:3: "Why do you look at the speck of sawdust in your brother's eye and pay no attention to the plank in your own eye?" Pursuing a greener life can quickly tailspin into finger pointing. Sadly, most of us find it easy to despise the logging industry or the oil companies while gassing up our cars and using paper. Before we campaign against all the ecological atrocities in our world, we need to understand why they happen and how our lifestyles literally fuel these disasters. Only then will the impact of greener personal choices trickle over to relieve the stresses these larger organizations place upon our planet. If we no longer want paper, that little blue logging machine can retire; the pudgy driver can get a job in wind energy.

That's Going to Leave a Mark

Everyone makes an impact on the world. It happens the moment we are born. As moms we know the little lives of our children make an enormous mark on our heart. The final weeks of pregnancy or an adoption process are brimming with conversations about anticipation and exhaustion. Many of us are not short on words to describe the anxiety of those last days, but we find ourselves instantly speechless when that baby is born. That exact moment is beyond words. It is never forgotten. Permanently etched into our minds and our souls, it is the moment we became something more than ourselves.

This is God's intricate design for humanity. His creativity

unleashed upon us has birthed a planet filled with fascinating people who are called to leave their fingerprints. God asks us to dream big and leave marks of love and compassion all over the place, like smudges on a stainless steel refrigerator, but when it comes to the earth, our God-designed impact needs to honor and preserve God's own creative process — creation. In other words, it needs to be simple. In Genesis 1 we were invited to be stewards of the earth. We were asked to partner with the planet to get only what we need from it and to care for and nurture the garden in the process. Sadly, we take more than we were ever given and leave a bigger mark than the earth can handle.

Just by Taking a Nap

Almost every activity we engage in has an impact on the planet. Take something as simple as sleeping. Think for a moment about how many chemicals and dyes were used to make your sheets. What material is your pillow composed of? How many pillows do you have? How much gas did it take to get the mattress to the store and then to your home? Was the alarm clock on the night stand made in China and shipped across the ocean? How much electricity does it take to run that clock? The night light? The heating and air conditioning that maintains a comfortable sleeping temperature? And who made all these materials? Were they paid a fair wage? Were they protected from dangerous pesticides or toxins? So many questions.

The amount of energy and resources it takes to create our stuff is staggering. From milk to polyester to computers, what we own makes an impact on our environment. Add to this what we do with what we own, and the impact multiplies. How far we drive those cars, how brightly we shine those lights, and how long we leave that refrigerator door open makes an impact. How hot we run our water, how often we run our dishwasher, and how long we keep our clothes matters to God's planet.

Each one of us places his or her personal mark on the earth at a different level. It is measured by what we have and how we use what we have. In this there are as many differences as there are individuals. How long you commute to work combined with what time you wake up and what you ate for lunch contributes to your own personal ecological impact. Banking online, living in a high rise, shopping locally, or driving an SUV can add or subtract from your personal impact.

Ecological Footprints

This impact is called your ecological footprint. There are many different footprints we make that, when combined, become our ecological footprint. The most comprehensive is our carbon footprint. A carbon footprint is the result of the carbon dioxide and other greenhouse gases that are released into the earth's atmosphere as a result of our lifestyles. Activities like driving, heating our homes, flying in a plane, and running our appliances contribute to our carbon footprint.

Another example of an ecological footprint is a water footprint, which is the impact our lives have on the water supply. It looks at how much water was used both directly and indirectly to bring us the goods and services we use. This includes the water we use to brush our teeth or nourish the lawn, but it also includes the water used in waste treatment and the manufacturing processes for items that we use.

Outside of our individual, ecological footprints, there are larger footprints that represent our families and the other organizations to which we belong. Every corporation and business has an ecological footprint, as do our homes. The schools and colleges in our communities as well as our recreation centers, governments, and churches have ecological footprints.

Now there are extremists who go to great lengths to avoid leaving any mark on the earth, but the reality is that we all leave an imprint simply by exhaling. Our green living goal is to uncover how damaging that mark is and how we can erase that damage. Ultimately, we'd like to see our footprint become as light as those of our kids when they run across a lawn. The blades of grass temporarily buckle, but they spring back quickly so you can hardly tell where our children have stepped.

What we don't want is a footprint like the one my son left when he took it upon himself to rearrange the landscaping in our backyard. He took a few discarded clay bricks that he found piled near the fence and set them in the grass behind the garage. They sat there for weeks. When I finally lifted the bricks to reset them on the stack, the grass underneath was yellowish brown and quite dead. The impact of this footprint was death to everything underneath.

Our hope when it comes to wise living is to reduce the impact of the footprints we place upon this planet. By converting our not-so-green behaviors into sustainable habits, we can reduce our ecological footprints. Our ultimate goal is to tread lightly. This is the place where many of the other changes we have discussed begin to add up to a softer step. When we limit our water use, walk instead of drive, clean with biodegradable products, and monitor our consumption, we begin to turn a combat boot into a flip-flop.

If you want to learn more about your specific ecological footprint before we go further into this discussion, log on to www.footprintnetwork.org and find the personal footprint calculator in the resources section. This will take you about ten minutes and will provide a summary of a few significant actions that determine the size of your family's footprint. You may find it helpful to know what sort of mark you are currently leaving as we move forward from here.

Those Footprints in the Sand

It's an odd thing to watch a toddler set his feet into the sand for the first time. As Midwesterners, the beach was not a part of our daily lives. So the first time we vacationed to a large coastal beach and put my son's clammy feet into the sand proved an interesting moment. My son was a bit particular, as many toddlers are, so intricacies like blades of grass and piles of sand that tickled were quite unnerving for him.

On this vacation we hauled him out to the beach and planted him squarely in the middle of a sea of sand hoping that his pudgy feet with curling toes would take to the soft beaches of central Mexico. This did not go over well. He gripped our hands as though we were about to be forever separated. With his palms locked into ours, he pulled his knees to his chest, attempting to defy gravity by simultaneously yanking both feet from the frightful sand.

This proved a bigger abdominal workout than his pouchy stomach was ready for, so he resorted to plan B, whining and hopping, trying his very best to step lightly. We continued to hold his hands as he looked at us with amazement that we had the audacity to let this travesty continue. We hesitated to rescue him immediately, as we were about to spend a week on the beach; our suitcases were jammed with pails and shovels, and sand was part of the plan. Eventually he gave up hopping and settled into a flamingo-like stance on one leg, still holding our hands. He hardly left a mark in that sand. He was so light and so desperate to get off the beach, that you could not tell where his feet had been.

Sometimes the best footprints are the ones we cannot see.

What Size Sandal Did Jesus Wear?

God did not call us to leave monster-sized shoeprints or tire tracks on the earth. He called us to simply leave the size six or size ten footsteps that he designed us with. Our footprints in the sand should leave plenty of beach for everyone else to walk. When we grab more than our share of the earth's resources, we become a bit bloated and our feet get swollen and cloddy. And when everyone else has big cumbersome feet, the beach is no longer fun.

Monitoring our ecological footprints means we leave behind the distinctive and creative mark God designed us to leave, and nothing else. People often attribute giant, marvelous things to God. This is theologically accurate. God is big and all-powerful; he's all encompassing. He's everywhere. He created the heavens and the earth. These are big things, but I think if Jesus were walking on the beach, he would still leave very small footprints.

God in flesh, Jesus Christ, was a simple carpenter, no elaborate house, no SUV, no vacation home on an island. His followers were utterly ordinary. His cup was simple and wooden. As a treasured teacher, he could have asked for more, but instead he gathered his followers around ordinary things, like a common meal and a loaf of bread. These were more than enough to satisfy their needs, and they are more than enough to satisfy ours.

He dressed simply and died all but naked. And while the Hellenistic world to which he ministered was two-thousand-years-ago different than ours, the desire to get more from life and leave a bigger mark were ever present, just as they are today. In all the extravagance of his world, Jesus lived simply and humbly. But, make no mistake, he left the biggest and greatest mark of all when he died on the cross and then triumphed over death.

It is quite possible to make a big mark yet leave behind a little one.

History has excavated and uncovered countless artifacts from almost all eras of human history. Great rulers left behind monuments and palaces, tombs and pyramids to mark their lives. Jesus left behind his words. The King of the Universe left his mark with stories about God. No elaborate tomb, no palace, no big footprint, just the most powerful words on the planet and an undeniable mark on our souls.

From Combat Boots to Flip-Flops

When it comes to a green life, moms can follow Jesus' model by putting into practice the green tips and tricks in this book and many other places to lower the amount of resources it takes to fuel their lives. Simply turning off unnecessary lights and walking to the post office instead of driving can shave a few centimeters off your footprint. However, there are some lifestyle habits that make a larger dent than others, so we've got to find creative ways to offset the cost of big-ticket ecological items.

Carbon offsets are one way that people creatively make up for the ecological damage their lifestyles incur. Try as we might to limit our travel, most of us will still jump on an airplane to visit Aunt Lil or Uncle Pat. And let's be honest, sometimes it is hard to shop locally, especially if you live in a rural area. Others of us live in communities with little or no public transportation, and we cannot afford a new hybrid. But never fear, you can still be a Green Mama with shrinking feet by buying carbon offsets for the times when a greener option is not available.

A carbon offset is a way to make a positive change for the earth to make up for the negative impact you made in another place. The basic idea is to offset the ecological damage of your not-so-green decision to fly to Toledo. Carbon offsets are not a free ticket to do whatever we please. The best decisions are still the ones that make little or no impact. Offsets are a bit like making an apology versus not making the mistake. Option A is to avoid the mistake, Option B is to apologize if the mistake has been made. Carbon offsets are like apologies to the planet.

Offsets are carbon credits that you buy from an organization specializing in making up to the planet. For example, air travel releases carbon dioxide into our atmosphere. So, to make up for your spring break trip to the sunshine, you can log onto a website that offers carbon credits and donate funds to a project that will plant trees in the Amazon.

Offsets can offer more to the earth than just planting trees. Many organizations selling carbon offsets are nonprofit groups that take your tax-deductible donation (which is your purchase of their offsets) and turn them loose to buy wind power, solar power, or relieve the damage from leaking landfills. There are offsets that help maintain trails, protect wildlife habitats, and restore areas ravaged by deforestation. Most organizations that provide offsets will list their projects, so you can choose the offset organization that works for your family by simply clicking onto a website and reading through the projects.

You are a busy mom with lots on your plate, so if logging on to find a carbon offset project seems a little daunting, think of it instead as a creative way to engage your kids in an ecological activity, a lesson on energy, or just a fun time on the computer looking at things like landfills and giant wind turbines. If your children are old enough, let them take charge of the offsets. Each week have one child take an hour to calculate the carbon your family spent that week, then determine how she wants to offset that impact. A list of organizations offering carbon offsets can be found in the Green Steps at the end of this chapter.

For some green folks, their goal is to live what is called a carbon-neutral or even a carbon-negative life. Meaning, they migrate toward habits that do not create carbon emissions at all and offset their impact when emissions are necessary. Today, many thoughtful organizations and companies are pursuing carbon offsets to this end. The Vatican is an intriguing example of this. It was the first truly carbon-neutral state. Choosing offsets works a bit like picking out a charity or fair-trade organization to support. You can make it engaging for your kids by choosing the projects and places that help them move forward with their One Big Thing.

As I ran down that Wisconsin highway (and at least I was running not driving) I began to understand why I always wanted to blame the catastrophe on someone else. I wanted to enjoy my tree-lined run and the newspaper. This is not possible. Our lives make an impact. Whenever we can, we need to minimize our damage, and in the places where we cannot, we should strive to offset it.

Green Steps

1. Read Low Carbon Diet by David Gershon (Empowerment Institute: Woodstock, N.Y., 2006).

This insightful resource for families looking to reduce their ecological footprint is a simple little workbook that is as user friendly as third-grade spelling homework. You can calculate your carbon footprint and find ways to reduce it. Also included are handy tips for helping organizations in your community lower their footprints, as well as a strategy for using it in a neighborhood (or a small group).

2. Visit a few trustworthy places to purchase carbon offsets.

Check out these websites for good offset programs: www.terrapass.com, www.carbonfund.org, www.nativeenergy.com.

Also, consider buying products from companies that either offset their emissions or make it easier for you to do so. For example, Dell and Volkswagen both offer programs to help you calculate and then donate toward offsetting the emissions from your car or the energy it takes to power your computer.

3. Continue on your campaign to decrease energy and water use in your home, workplace, church, etc.

Share your mission and reason for doing this with your neighbors, coworkers and others you encounter on a regular basis. Your example can help others decrease their footprint. Sometimes it helps to advertise what we do and why we do it.

Your Eco-Examen for Chapter 7

❑ What is one area where you might consider offsetting in your family?

❑ Where is one place that offsets do not work for your family?

Working the System:
Purchasing Power

Religion that God our Father accepts as pure and faultless is this:
to look after orphans and widows in their distress.
JAMES 1:27

When businesses don't pay a living wage all society pays.
We pay through poverty and needless disease,
disability and death from inadequate health care.
We pay as women struggle to put food on the table. We pay
as businesses and communities suffer economic decline.
MARGOT DORFMAN, CEO, US WOMEN'S CHAMBER OF COMMERCE

My friend Lynn once took me to the Ravenswood neighborhood on Chicago's north side, where she introduced me to a fabulous little organization called the Enterprising Kitchen. It's nothing fancy, just warehouse space and a few small offices. From the outside it looks like any other urban industrial building turned trendy loft space. Cool bricks, exposed ductwork, a coffee shop nearby.

Once inside, however, it is apparent this is no ordinary kitchen. It smells like a spa. Warm air with a tinge of lavender and mint pry open your senses. Racks of elegant candles tucked into tawny baskets fill the stockroom. The day we visited, small groups of women were cutting and wrapping rows of glycerin soaps with cellophane and an aromatherapy twist.

The Enterprising Kitchen is a nonprofit organization that helps unemployed and underemployed women gain the workplace skills they need to support themselves and their families. Here, women with little or no formal education can learn. Women with shabby job skills can receive training. Women whose dignity has been crushed can earn a paycheck. Here, a simple bar of soap makes a big difference.

Their products are handmade by the women employed at the Kitchen and come from sources as close to nature as possible. All the proceeds go back to empowering more women and rebuilding more lives. This small but mighty group of women manage to stock their products in three hundred stores throughout the country (www .theenterprisingkitchen.org).

The year Lynn and I made our visit was the year I vowed that all my Christmas gifts would help others. Why grab soap from some lame store in the mall when I could give a bar that changes lives? My tea-sipping friends would get fair-trade teas. My hippie friends would get handmade bags from Guatemala and earrings from Cape Town. If I had friends that loved soaps and candles, I would buy them from places like the Enterprising Kitchen.

My little excursion with Lynn opened my eyes to the whole idea of giving gifts for good. Of course, like so many other things in life, that Christmas did not go exactly as I had planned. Turns out there was not a Lego helicopter that would benefit a worthy cause, and candy canes really benefit no one. But since that day, etched into my mind is a rule I live by.

Whenever possible I make my purchases count.

It's about More than Trees

At first glance, the green conversation may appear to be mostly about organic food and saving trees, but a sustainable life is one that benefits more than just virgin forests. A truly green life seeks to build healthy families, communities, campuses, churches, and marketplaces. It seeks to build a better world. The sort of world I think Jesus would advocate. It benefits the buyer and the seller, the farmers and the people of their villages. It benefits teachers, pastors, parks, pools, recreation centers, clerks, salespeople, truck drivers, waste haulers, and of course, the trees.

A truly sustainable and planet-friendly life will take everyday tasks like drinking coffee and getting dressed, and whenever possible, turn them into ways to make a difference. This may mean drinking your coffee from a mug handmade by a local artist. And it can mean even more when that coffee or tea was fairly traded, helping the grower feed his family and earn an honest wage. It might also mean taking a morning shower and using soap from the Enterprising Kitchen.

The Caffeine Buzz

I managed to make it through college unfazed by the cloud of caffeine addiction that hovered over most students I knew. Like a fourth grader sipping from her mom's cup, I made several over-dramatic sputters and gasps if I even took one sip of coffee. But eventually the little brown bean did get me. One afternoon during my mid-twenties, determined to grow up and overcome by an urge to be trendy, I ventured into a local coffee shop.

I was a nervous coffee neophyte and have to admit that I was even sweating as I stood staring at the menu board. I did not recognize any of the listed items. They were expensive and sounded Italian or

French, and it turns out I had only learned Spanish. A businessman who looked like he knew how to order coffee stood behind me. I panicked at the thought that he would silently mock my rookie drink order.

When it was my turn, I ordered a large mocha. Of course the snippy barista could not resist her temptation to correct me. "You mean a venti?" she huffed.

"Yes, yes, a venti, I'll have a venti mocha," I quickly corrected myself.

Today I've become quite the coffee connoisseur. I no longer need a fancy drink, just dark roast coffee with lots of cream, and always a venti. I'm hyped from my little cup of morning gold for most of the day. I'm not sure this is a good thing, as it makes me talk way too fast, but it also helped me survive those bleary-eyed early newborn days.

Many folks I know hit the coffee pot on a regular basis. We are part of a national coffee obsession. The United States is the largest purchaser of coffee on the planet, consuming one-fifth of all the coffee grown in the world. Coffee is clearly part of the daily routine for millions of Americans, which makes it a great place to begin the conversation on how our purchases can make a difference.

Throughout the world, many small coffee growers find themselves competing with large, corporately owned farms that grow coffee and other crops on a massive scale. These corporate crops are sold at prices significantly cheaper than what small family growers can offer. Obviously this undercuts the small farms and threatens to shove them out of business. So (and I realize this is dramatically simplifying the complex economic and social issues involved) intermediaries, often called "coyotes" have stepped in to buy coffee from these small farmers at low prices. These prices can be substantially lower than the farmer could have originally sold for, were it not for the competition of the large farms. But because of the large farms,

the only options become selling low to the go-between or not selling at all.

With enough small growers in their network, these middle players can compete with the large farms and make big money for themselves. The losing end of these transactions are the small farmers,
who, in many places, sell for such a small price they become indebted
to these coyotes and a cycle of poverty and debt follows. Entire communities can crumble and find themselves chained to corporations
and middle players. Which means their families receive shabby or
no health care; children are left with no education, or worse, find
themselves enslaved; and standards of living dip to levels unknown
by most of the Western world.

Fair prices help keep small farmers and the communities they
are a part of intact. This simple fact is not rocket science, yet many
companies ignore it. Others are stepping in to support these small
growers throughout the world. Fair-trade is the label these empowering companies place on their method of doing business. It hardly
seems fair to destroy an entire community for a cup of cheap coffee.

Along with paying fair prices, fair trade also means that workers
are treated with dignity and respect. Child labor is prohibited. Many
fair-trade companies help fund local education and social programs
for the communities where their products are grown. They believe
the families involved in the process matter. Fair-trade products are
usually manufactured with ecological integrity and are harvested
with an eye toward sustainability and preservation of the environment. Many mission organizations throughout the world support
fair-trade communities in their areas.

Now, if we pause for a moment and reread this definition of
fair trade, we find support for many of the social issues that matter to Jesus. Throughout the Bible we find encouragement to care
for the poor and to promote justice: "For I, the Lord, love justice; I
hate robbery and iniquity" (Isa. 61:8); "let justice roll on like a river,

righteousness like a never-failing stream!" (Amos 5:24). And from the oft quoted Micah 6:8 we know that what the Lord requires of us is "to act justly and to love mercy and to walk humbly with your God."

So when we hear a call to honesty and business practices that lean on integrity rather than the bottom line, we are hearing an invitation to support the cause of justice. Supporting fair-trade products is more than just another trendy green maneuver. It is a lifestyle tweak that brings a bit of Jesus' passion home to the kitchen table and the coffee pot. It helps us empower people and pursue the heart of Jesus through our everyday lives.

This matters to God.

So by simply brewing fair-trade coffee (and caffeine fans can rejoice; there are lots to choose from) we can enrich the lives of families in places we may never see. Visit Grounds for Change (www .groundsforchange.com) to find an overview of some fair-trade coffees. Also, check your local coffee shop for recommendations. Many chains and brands also offer fair-trade options (Starbucks, Peets, and Green Mountain are a few).

And Chocolate Too?

If coffee with integrity is not enough to make you jittery, another place to make a big difference through seemingly everyday items is in the world of chocolate. Like coffee growers, cacao farmers face devastating social and political scenarios while trying to eke out a living.

Our Halloween treats and Valentine's hearts come at a hefty price. Forty percent of the world's cacao beans come from Côte d'Ivoire (Ivory Coast). Here, child labor is commonplace on family farms and plantations. But not necessarily by choice. In a world where poverty reigns supreme, the only option many of these families have is to set their kids to work the fields rather than go to school. There is little education, health care, or help for these families who cannot afford the basics. Paying them more for their cacao woud greatly enhance their quality of life, but sometimes life turns out to be more about the bottom line.

The International Institute of Tropical Agriculture estimates that in Nigeria, Cameroon, Côte d'Ivoire, and Ghana, children earn roughly $80 annually for their work on a cacao plantation. Over 80 percent have never attended school, and instead, perform dangerous labor for our national sweet tooth. Roughly 152,000 children apply pesticides (often without proper protection). And 146,000 children under age fifteen clear plantations with machetes. In Côte d'Ivoire, chocolate companies signed on to end child labor in the chocolate industry by 2005.[1] That date was later changed to 2008, where, once again, many deadlines went unmet. I am no longer able to enjoy a chocolate heart or a simple chocolate square without thinking of the fact that an eight-year-old is sitting around cracking open cacao beans when she could be in school if her family earned a fair wage for that chocolate.[2]

If it was not fairly traded, it is likely tainted. Now I suspect that I have ruined chocolate for you too.

So what's a Green Mama to do?

Look for chocolate products with a conscience. If we are going to dive into the extra calories and swim down the dessert aisle, let's make it count! Skip the questionable products and look for fair-trade bars that do more than wreck our chances of fitting into our skinny jeans. Green and Black's is a great bar, by their calculations, giving growers a 25 percent premium on their product and only raising the price we pay for their bar by 4 percent (www.greenandblacks. com).[3] Dagoba is one of the premier fair-trade chocolate companies with some exotic blends that include rosehip and lavender (www .dagobachocolate.com). Equal Exchange Chocolate is another great place to find chocolate that makes a difference (www.shop.equalex change.com). These options are available at most organic grocers, many national grocery chains, and on occasion, big-box retailers like Target. Ordering them online is always an option, and, yes, it adds to our carbon footprint by shipping it, but the not-so-fair-trade chocolate was shipped to your stores as well.

You will notice it may cost a few bucks more to satisfy that sweet tooth, but the reward is all the more meaningful. You get a great bar of chocolate, and families in places like Côte d'Ivoire and Ghana get a fair wage. The planet also gets a break.

There is a reason those other bars are so cheap.

Savvy Consumers

I learned a lot about labels when I started junior high. As I entered sixth grade in the mid-eighties, I thought I was the snappiest girl in that school. I had a pair of white overalls splattered with neon paint. Bright gold socks and white sneakers balanced out a pair of enormous, square orange earrings. I thought this was the very best outfit on the planet. No one else had this fabulous getup.

Guess jeans were what everyone else was wearing. The original Guess jeans, the ones with the red and white triangle label on the back pocket. They were expensive, they were trendy, and I did not have a pair. I started sixth grade blissfully unaware of Guess jeans. I only had eyes for splatter paint. Labels did not mean a thing to me. If only adolescence in the US could stay that way. However, once I discovered this designer denim, my middle-school world changed.

No longer would my one-of-a-kind flea-market overalls do. I needed Georges Marciano's jeans, and Gloria Vanderbilt's too. I became a name-brand junkie and have been weaning myself from this obsession ever since. I can read labels from a mile away. Many of us can. Perhaps we no longer fret over designer denim, but we all know who makes the most expensive stroller or sleeper sets. Designer diaper bags are a multi-million-dollar business. So is children's outerwear and footwear, other places those labels are evident to all. Even if we wisely choose not to chase after these trinkets, many moms know what they are.

So what might it look like if we twisted our label radars to track fair-trade goods rather than designer goods? What if a fair-trade logo made our hearts leap the way a Forenza sweater did in 1988? In a way that is similar to organic labeling, fair-trade organizations have a label system that is helpful to follow. However, unlike the support organic labels receive from the US government, there is not currently a federally monitored labeling system for fair-trade products.

To make up for this missing link, several organizations through whom many fairly traded products can receive credibility have emerged. TransFair USA is among the most prominent and offers certification on products like coffee and tea, fresh flowers, fruit, herbs, vanilla, and, of course, chocolate. If you see their label, you know that the product has been fair-trade certified (www.transfair USA.org).

This is not the only way to find fair-trade products. If you simply scan through the lists of missionary and microfinance organizations in your community, church, or denomination, you will discover that if you need to make a purchase, you can find several goods for good all on your own. Popcorn from the Boy Scouts and cookies from the Girl Scouts all count toward these efforts.

Every year campaigns for breast cancer research and other diseases receive a portion of the sales on many products. Most shoppers instantly recognize that famous pink ribbon printed across everything from tennis balls to yogurt. Buying these products can make a difference.

In 2006, major retailers like the Gap, American Express, Hallmark, Microsoft, Apple, and several others joined to embark upon the Red Campaign. Whenever you purchase a "Red" item from one of these retailers, they will contribute up to 50 percent of their profits for antiretroviral drugs that will alleviate the suffering of those struggling with HIV and AIDS in Africa. The Red Campaign website (www.joinred.com) explains the campaign as a partnership between desire and virtue. If people desire an item, their purchases can have virtue when they bring power to help in places like Rwanda and Swaziland.

Turns out there are many avenues for making your purchases count. Just be sure to reflect before you buy, even when it is for a good cause. For example, when buying something we need, campaigns like Red are the way to go. You need an item, the Global Fund (which is where the Red proceeds go) needs money. Everybody wins. But when we are out having a frivolous moment (like the time I was in Dallas and bought camouflage cowboy boots), we have to ask what is better, buying the $50 Red sweatshirt that sends $5 of the profit to Africa, or skipping the purchase to send the whole $50 to Africa? Do we really *need* that sweatshirt (or those boots)?

Thoughtful products should not replace thoughtful spending!

Shop Close to Home

Whenever possible, shop locally; it helps fuel thoughtful spending as well. If you have the choice between picking up a pair of pajamas from the big-box store on the corner, where the profits go to an unknown corporate entity you will never directly encounter, or purchasing the pj's from a small store owned by a local businesswoman, shop the local gal if you can. It is better for her and for your neighborhood. You've helped a local woman keep her doors open, which in turn helps your community through everything from tax dollars for your schools to maintaining rental prices in your downtown area. A vibrant town or city center is one sign of a healthy community.

When local shops close up, property values dip, and communities take the hit. The big store with all the fluorescent lights and no windows really does not care about this, so why shop there if you can help it? Sometimes this is tough; in many places the local stores are more expensive or nonexistent (often pushed out of business by the bigger stores). Still, whenever possible, shop locally.

Eating locally is the same game. I will always try to visit the locally owned Mediterranean Cafe in my town long before I go grab a salad at a national chain restaurant. Local restaurants offer unique dishes that have been inspired by someone down the street or by their Grandma Sandy's pasta sauce, rather than from corporate head-quarters clear across the country. And you can find local options that offer seasonal cuisine that is served up fresh from farm produce a few counties over. These are not options on most chain restaurant menu boards.

Another example is to pick up your produce, herbs, baked goods, or flowers from a local farmer's market. Of course, again, the best of the best here would be to grow and make your own, but most moms struggle to make a garden their primary food source. Local markets are a win for you and the farmer. Prices are usually cheaper, you meet the guy who grew the watermelon, and you have supported your local economy. You've probably saved on gas and emissions as well. The farmer only has to truck the food to town, and then you take it home. There are no ocean freighters or diesel-guzzling semi-trucks involved. No strawberries from South America. Just you and the guy from across the county.

More than simply shopping local, you can work the food system by choosing to eat less meat. According to Frances Moore Lappe in her book "Diet for a Small Planet," it takes roughly 16 pounds of grain and soy feed to yield one pound of meat. Each grain-consuming animal that we fatten up to be consumed will eat roughly 2.5 tons of grain and other feed each year.

What this means, is that for every one pound of meat, we are say-ing adios to sixteen pounds of perfectly edible grain. Plant-derived foods are a clear winner when considering how to work the food system. According to Lappe, those sixteen pounds of grain have twenty-one times the calories and eight times the protein than a one-pound burger.[4]

By simply choosing to skip meat for one meal per day or a few days per week, we can make an enormous impact on the planet. You do not have to become a vegetarian, but passing on the burger once in a while is better for your heart and for the planet.

Ultimately, when we recognize that our purchases have power, we can begin to make an impact on the world simply by choosing wisely where we spend our money.

Green Steps

1. Consider one-for-one organizations.

Consider organizations that donate an item for every item purchased. TOMS Shoes is a good example (www.tomsshoes.com). TOMS promises to send one pair of shoes to a needy child for every one pair they sell. You buy a pair, they send a pair. You can also give these as gifts with an email that offers a link to the TOMS Shoes website. Here the recipient of your gift can watch what TOMS calls a "shoe drop," where you can watch them distribute the shoes across the world.

2. Consider fair-trade toys.

A reputable company offering fair-trade toys is World of Good (www.worldofgood.com). Here you will find a solid selection of hand-made toys whose profits directly benefit the families manufacturing them. What you will not find here are pages of light-up toys that whiz and whirl like many American toys do. Many of these toys have a distinct look and feel compared to the mainstream gadgets. What a great way to introduce your kids to other cultures, bringing both the educational and the social benefit of these products home.

3. Host a party.

Every month I am invited to some sort of home party where a myriad of gadgets are sold. Women today sell everything from baskets to cookware to candles, makeup, and jewelry. The gathering includes time to chat, time to eat, but also a presentation and a call to open your wallet. These events are helpful to many who are trying to supplement their family's income.

The success of these projects prompts the suggestion that a mom might also consider hosting a party where the proceeds and products benefit microfinance or fair-trade organizations. A mom can buy items from one of these organizations and host a party to educate others about the causes and sell merchandise that benefits other women and families in need.

Take, for example, my friend who works for an organization in Cape Town called Farflung. She runs a training program for women with design and handcraft skills, with an emphasis on empowering them through microenterprise. These women, through this program, create art and products to be sold under the Farflung brand. All the proceeds go to helping these women support their families.

There are thousands of projects like this throughout the world. Ten Thousand Villages (www.tenthousandvillages.com) is a great place to connect with products and people from around the world. Consider shopping for necessary gifts and presents from a site like this. You, as a mom, can help another mom by simply making your purchases through a thoughtful site like this.

There are also several companies that sell beads and jewelry-making materials that are fairly traded. Without much effort a mom could host her own jewelry party to benefit other communities. Simply order a variety of beads and items from these organizations. Invite a friend with some jewelry skills into the loop. Set out the beads and call your friends. You can set a small price for the beads, and once again, everyone wins. Your friends go home with a cute little bracelet and families in poverty get a boost. Looking for beads? Check out Bead for Life (www.beadforlife.org). They even have a link for women who want to host a party.

Your Eco-Examen for Chapter 8

☐ What is one way that I make my purchases count?

☐ What is one place where it would be hard to have my purchases count?

9

Green Traditions:
Celebrating Holidays and Special Days

They [family traditions] help us define who we are;
they provide something steady,
reliable and safe in a confusing world.
SUSAN LIEBERMAN, *NEW TRADITIONS*

For the Lord is good and his love endures forever;
his faithfulness continues through all generations.
PSALM 100:5

I once met a hiker whose job it was to march to the top of Colorado's highest peaks. He worked for the US Geological Survey and needed to calculate their exact position, confirming that the information driving today's GPS technology was correct. He spent his days on the summits of soaring mountains, soaking up the view from fourteen thousand feet. I met him while hiking myself; I was simply having a weekend warrior moment and would return to a desk on Monday. He got to do this all the time.

Because of all our techy gadgets, including the GPS he was somehow calibrating, I don't actually have to drag myself up these peaks to know anything about them. All I need to do is punch a few buttons, and my laptop or even my cell phone can tell me the elevation of almost every peak in the world. I can also get a view from the top via Google Earth, and I can do this all from my couch without ever getting close to the Rocky Mountains.

Unless I determine otherwise, I am separated from God's creation.

As I have studied the Scriptures, I have noticed that the stories of God's people, unlike my current story, are intimately linked with creation. God's people had to know something of the earth to survive, and they kept their eye on nature because they knew God revealed himself there. Take for example Moses, who consistently met with God in the natural world. From burning bushes to clouds descending on Mt. Sinai, his experience of God came through creation.

The Israelites camped out in the wilderness for forty years. Each night they were acutely aware of their vulnerable position as the predators and dangers of their wild places closed in on them. Each day they could know more of God's provision as they received nourishment from the earth.

Mary and Joseph walked a long dusty road on Christmas Eve. They were outside. No minivan, no heater or air-conditioning, just groaning livestock and God's big sky.

Peter stuck his big old feet into the sea when he stepped out of that boat. Paul probably traveled over 10,000 miles on his missionary journeys. He spent these miles bouncing along the Roman landscape or rolling across the open sea; he did not fly to Corinth.

For most of human history, people could not consult the Weather Channel for the local forecast, so they learned to read the sky and watch the clouds. They did not have access to a GPS that could deposit them at their cousin's doorway, so they learned to identify landmarks or read maps. Sailors were trained to read the stars. In our marvelously sophisticated lives, where much of our discovering is done for us, we can lose our sense of awe and wonder at the natural world if we do not intentionally immerse ourselves in the outdoors.

We need to move beyond the coordinates and into the actual places God created. Weaving a green element into our family traditions is one creative way to accomplish this.

Family traditions are a great time to make some eco-friendly changes that draw your family closer to creation. Because they are recurring, the green tweaks that you make to your traditions will remind you year after year of the joy to be found in nature and the hope we hold in preserving it.

A Simple Wreath, A Powerful Reminder

Making our traditions greener begins by asking ourselves where we find the natural world in our special family moments. Don't fret, you will not need to add a camping trip to your New Year's plans or move the birthday party to the beach, unless you want to do so. Greener traditions can be easy to make. Ultimately, we want our traditions to stay pretty much the same anyway — this is, after all, what makes them traditions. We just want to start noticing the natural world along the way.

Take for example the tradition of hanging a holiday wreath. Many Christian denominations celebrate Advent. Advent is the season leading us to Christmas, four Sundays that mark the coming of the Christ Child. Stemming from the tradition of the Advent wreath, millions of families hang a wreath on their door, garage, or even the front grill of their cars during this time of year.

Gertrud Mueller Nelson in her book *To Dance with God* recalls one version of the history behind these decorative wreaths. According to Nelson, ancient peoples who lived in the far northern climates were acutely aware of the cold and darkness that settled into their lives each winter. As days grew icy and nights became longer, separation from the warmth of the sun changed their way of approaching each day. With daylight diminished, their lives were not as productive as during the height of summer. Life slowed down.

Rather than fight this reality (the way we do today with electricity), they succumbed to God's world and minimized their outdoor activity. One way of marking this seasonal shift and surrendering to this new pace was to remove the wheels from their wagons and carts, bring them inside, and decorate them with greens and candles. This decorative wheel was a symbol settling them into the necessary slowing of their lives.

Think for a moment of how our little frenetic worlds would change if we popped the front tire off our car and slapped it on the kitchen table. We would feel shipwrecked, of course. But in the candles that decorated this wheel all winter, perhaps we might also find a reminder that soon enough, the warmth of sunlight and hyperactivity would return.[1]

Today we pull up to a tree lot, with our wheels firmly in place, toss a hoop of fresh evergreen into the trunk, and head home to tack it to the door. With the busyness of the Christmas season, hanging a wreath might mark the beginning of the most harried time of year rather than a season to slow down and wait. In our culture, December is so *not* the month to remove a tire, but in the season of Christmas and Advent, God really is calling us to take a break and wait for his Son's entry into this world. Advent means the arrival of something long awaited.

So where is the green moment in this tradition? It comes when we see a wreath and think of God's invitation to slow things down rather than dash out for last-minute gifts. Christmas festivities can be greener if we are reminded of the seasons in our natural world when we see a wreath (or a tree or boughs of holly and mistletoe too). Christmas is more sustainable if we truly give in to this invitation to slow down by driving less and buying less. Which can translate into a decrease in packaging, spending, longing, and consuming. Which triggers a smaller trash can and less junk carted off to our landfills. Which means less pollution to get our trash there and less seepage into our groundwater, and on it goes.

All because you were reminded of the heart of God behind that wreath on the door.

In other holidays and seasonal changes we can find these green opportunities. In North America Easter coincides with the warmth of spring. As we see new life eager to burst forth, we celebrate the new life we find in Christ. After the gray slush of winter and Lent have passed, we celebrate the brilliant colors of spring. When we set aside the plastic eggs and chocolate bunnies to consider for a moment how hard it must be for the crocus to push its way through the frozen dirt, we catch a glimpse of how grueling it must have been for Jesus to push forward for us.

Easter traditions become greener when we notice creation in them.

Adding a Green Element

Most of us are familiar with the idea of adding a little educational piece to our traditions when it comes to Christmas. Without constant reminders of the reason we celebrate Christmas, our kids will become overzealous Santa Claus fanatics, so most moms I know try to educate their children about the deeper meaning of Christmas. The advent of Jesus into this world calls us into the stable where the Savior of the world rests on his mother's chest and waits. We pray and sing "O Come, O Come, Emmanuel," and we know that, despite the insatiable appetite of this season, God is with us as his bigger story hangs in the air. So we read of Mary and Joseph, and we sprinkle all the visits to men in red suits with real stories of life and love as they come from God.

In a similar way, lessons on creation care can be sprinkled into all our celebrations throughout the year, especially in those places where finding something green to pull out is difficult. Look for places to drop in an eco-lesson for your children. Is there a special day or season of the year when it seems fitting for your family to plant a tree? Is there a family member no longer living whose memory a special plant could preserve?

Adding trees or shrubs to your own yard, or to a nearby park through a local conservation program, can become a lesson on life and growth. Next time a birthday or holiday pops up and your kids suddenly find themselves buried under gadgets they will soon forget, take them outside to check out their tree. Give everyone a breath of fresh air and a break from plastic packaging.

Wrap them up and haul them outside on Christmas Eve and look for the brightest star. As you gaze across the silent sky on this holy night, the story of the Magi suddenly comes to life. Find a chart of the stars and follow a constellation across the sky as the seasons change. Make a point of staying up late to catch a lunar eclipse or a glimpse of Venus. Stargazing on these uncommon nights might be a new tradition for your family, especially if you live in a rural community where you are blessed to actually see so many of the stars.

If we want our children to know more of God through our traditions, we should always try to consider ways to add these natural elements. Now here is where some of my friends will quip that adding eco-flair to the holidays is easier for me because I happen to crave opportunities to be outside and to camp or take a hike. I have several adorable friends who would rather sit on a searing-hot marshmallow skewer than sleep in a tent.

Others will only bother to hike if they know they can soak in a nearby hot tub once the whole walking part is over. I also know people who would take a day at the spa over a canoe trip anytime. These are not bad things, and, as much as I love dipping into the woods, I must confess that planting gardens and shrubs and trees is a challenge for me. I never know which tree to choose or how deep the hole is supposed to be, and I am racked with guilt should the poor twig not survive.

But whether we consider ourselves "outdoorsy people" or not, we are called to know more about God and engage God's creation. So along with the other spiritual disciplines we may engage in, like going to church, reading the Bible, praying, and communing with the people of God, spending time in the creation of God is essential to our souls. God chose to express himself through the natural world, so we need to know this world.

Your Own Unique Family Traditions

As moms, we are eager for our families to have a sense of tradition that is unique just to them. In our quirky little rituals we can immerse our families in the past they never knew and can make a mark on the future where we will not be present. When my kids eat my apple pie, they are eating the same pie their great-grandmother, who they will never meet, baked. When I pass on the seventy-five-year-old rolling pin that flattened the dough of these pies, my sons or daughter will grip the same worn red handles my grandmother held. I am passing along our own unique memories.

When I was in high school, our family took a vacation through Georgia. My memories of this trip are mostly of the adolescent vacation variety. My sister and I sleeping in the back of our van as we zipped down the interstate. Mom and Dad debating directions. Camping out and toasting s'mores. Singing along with Kenny Rogers.

As we drove across the rural sections of the state, we quickly discovered that the famed Georgia peaches were in season. I've never had a thick, luscious peach the size of a twelve-inch softball until I visited Georgia. They soon became our vacation obsession. So much so that when it came time to head back north, we realized we could not bear the thought of a day without them. So on our way out of the state, we packed our van with a bushel basket full of furry little fruits. We even laid out a comforter and tucked each peach into its own puff of blanket so it could smoothly ride all the way to Chicago.

At home, these peaches were served up as our family's favorite delicacy, inexorably linking memories of that trip to a tradition already long held by our family: peach dumplings. Twice a year my mom made them. Only in the summer, because that was their season, and only when we begged her endlessly. Wrapped in thick, floury dough, the peaches were boiled, then drizzled with the perfect mixture of butter, cinnamon, and sugar. The next day my sister and I would fight over the leftovers and then settle in to wait for dumpling time to come around again. From my grandmother to my mom and now on to my kids, this is our summer tradition. A tradition rooted in sugar and fruit trees.

What are the most treasured traditions in your family? Certain photographs repeated every year? A special breakfast on the first day of school? An heirloom ornament or an autumn bonfire? For many of us, our sense of family is inseparable from these annual moments. As the days slip off our calendars, events that once seemed ordinary come to be sacred. After time, something as simple as peach dumplings can remind us of who we are and what our story is. Tradition roots us in the past so that it can illuminate the present.

Tradition can also root us in God's creation, illuminating the Creator.

The Irony of Traditions

Ironically, if we set out to preserve our apple pies and sweet sixteen parties without an eye on the environment, we harm the very lives we are hoping to enhance. After we discover the big picture of God's creation shining through our traditions, we need to begin greening up the details as well. Otherwise, the number of generations to whom we can pass on our traditions becomes alarmingly few. So let's begin· to ask ourselves if Christmas always has to be wrapped in paper and if we have to start shopping at 3:00 a.m. on the day after Thanksgiving. And do ten-year-old boys really notice the super cute birthday napkins we set out for them?

Two of my children have summer birthdays near the Fourth of July holiday. Exhausted by the idea of again filling trash bags with paper plates and plastic flatware, I set out to host an eco-friendly birthday party for my sons. Metal plates in red, white, and blue were flanked by patriotic cloth napkins and reusable flatware. Of course the serving trays matched as well. I was quite proud of myself that day — still am. As I set the table for our party, I was already twenty years' worth of birthdays ahead of myself. I thought about the fact that these items would outlive me and possibly outlive my children. All the items on our table could be used year after year.

Like a sap I had visions of my boys using these plates and forks for their own kids. I rambled on to my husband, wondering which child would take off with these plates once we died. Would they fight over them? More likely, they would become the odd plates Mom always used and the napkins she refused to part with. Either way, we started a greener tradition that day. We had party ware for the next half century and would not buy paper birthday plates again.

Begin at the Birthday

Do you have a tradition you can green up? If you find yourself staring at the calendar and wondering where to start, you might find birthdays are a simple way to begin. Most moms I know make a fuss over their children's birthdays. Whether it involves a large party at a theme park or a simple meal at home, this is a special day.

The reason we do this whole green thing is to make the lives of those we love healthier and stronger. The trees are not the point, the people who get to play, work, and live in the shade of those trees are the point. So it makes sense that the one day a year when you stop to cherish life would also be the day you vow to make the world that life will inherit better. Greener.

It is easy to get dragged into the details of a birthday and overlook the wild potential in these days. I've had many friends sheepishly admit that the day they throw a party for one of their kids is the day their stress level reaches cataclysmic heights. They confess they are edgy and tense; they roar when milk from breakfast splatters across the floor. "Be careful!" they shriek. "Don't you know we are having people over today?"

As they charge off to the grocery store to pick up the ice cream, they bark orders to everyone left at home, and the very child they strive to honor gets overlooked. So what are we really trying to celebrate? All the gimmicks and gadgets that go into a fabulous party? The accolades we receive from our children or friends once it is over, or the reality that the God of the universe dipped his pinky finger into our lives and created anew the hope for tomorrow in each of our children? Be diligent about celebrating what is important, and it will end up triggering a more sustainable birthday.

Greening up birthdays is one way to force us out of the details, since it asks us to leave behind the gadgetry, and delve into the moment. If we start by making these celebrations of life a little greener, eventually the eco-friendly tweaks will infiltrate the rest of our traditions. A significant list of ideas on how to green up a birthday can be found in the Green Steps section of this chapter.

Back to the Too Much Stuff

Remember our conversation in chapter 4 about all our stuff? What might it look like to go for a gift-free Christmas or birthday those first two years of your child's life? Call me a scrooge, but other than an ornament, I did not give any of my children a gift for Baby's First Christmas. My daughter was just three weeks old on her first Christmas; she did not know she had feet, let alone understand how cute a pink beret and matching sweater could be.

A great family I know asked the guests at their daughter's first birthday to consider making a donation to a charity on her behalf along with or in lieu of bringing a gift. They selected a ministry that provided healthcare and medicine to sick children living in poverty. For the first year of her life, this baby girl gave the gift of life to kids she will likely never meet this side of heaven. The celebration of her birthday was an opportunity to give others the chance to celebrate a few more birthdays. I wish I had thought of this.

As our kids get older, we all know going giftless becomes exceptionally challenging. My oldest starts his 364-day birthday countdown the morning after his most recent party. Kids love presents. Heck, I love presents. To suggest that an eight-year-old skip out on gifts is hard.

Instead, encourage moderation. Consider donating duplicate gifts or unwanted toys to a charity rather than racing back to Toys 'R' Us with the gift receipts. In our family I set aside some of the trinkets my children do not need, as well as the duplicate toys we receive throughout the year, and add them to a shoebox that will serve as a Christmas present for a child living in poverty. The Operation Christmas Child program through Samaritan's Purse (www.samaritanspurse.org) offers you a chance to do the same. We pack these toys in with toothbrushes and school supplies, and suddenly we have gifts for children in the Philippines. And my children never miss the new toys they add to the boxes.

Another good friend gives only useful items as party favors. She packs little boxes of soaps, toothpaste, wash cloths, and lotion for all the party goers who come to her house.

When you do buy gifts, ask yourself if you really need to purchase a spanking new toy or gadget. My oldest happens to think that when a gift comes in the mail without all the official packaging (like from eBay or Craigslist) it is far superior to one from the store. Why? Because someone already did all the work of taking it out of the package. And we all know that taking a toy out of a package can rival most visits to the gym with the number of twist ties and hoops and loops that must be cut and stretched to get a simple toy out of its plastic. He thinks someone did him a huge favor if he gets an unwrapped gadget. Buy it used if you can.

You can also simply reuse or recycle the packaging on gifts you do buy new, and whenever possible, invite your kids into conversations about why we give and receive gifts. Help them keep a wider, more global perspective on material goods. This conversation is especially poignant in times of economic hardship. Slim giving is good giving.

All Wrapped Up
with No Place to Go

So what to do about that wrapping paper? It's so lovely, and with the perfect bow, it tells the recipient how lucky she is that we came to her party. And what kid does not love a package covered with pictures of princesses or tree frogs? Adorable as it may be, wrapping paper (and those cute little gift bags too) are phenomenally unnecessary.

Most of these papers are filled with toxic ink and never see the inside of a recycling bin. They can even contain lead, metal-based foils, or chlorine. If you happen to host a perfect little Currier and Ives Christmas complete with a roaring fire, tossing your wrapping paper into that fire emits a cloud of toxic fumes for your kids to breathe.

My life is hectic enough that I've slapped tape and paper onto a gift in the car at the red lights on the way to a party. Less than two hours after wrapping perfect, brand new paper around a box, it is wallowing at the bottom of a Hefty bag in a balled-up inky mess, right next to a deflated drink box. There has to be a better way to help a gift go incognito.

Here are a few paperless options. First, consider buying kid-friendly pillowcases. You can place gifts in pillowcases, tie a reusable ribbon around the top (especially for girls, they can later use them on their hair) and you now have a paperless gift. You can also give your friends a present "wrapped" in a canvas bag they can reuse at the grocery store or library. Hostess gifts look lovely in handmade baskets. Consider stocking a supply from a microfinance project in another country, where proceeds benefit people in a local village (see www.opportunity.org for a great explanation of and way to get involved with these sorts of projects).

If you cannot fight the urge to wrap it, is there anything else lying around you can pad the little present with? My brother-in-law used to wrap our Christmas gifts in his physics homework. Used magazines or comics have a similar effect and you can recycle both when the unwrapping ends. Old butcher block paper can become a creative wrap after your kids doodle and stamp it. If your child has an easel, the used paper from that is a good size for gift wrap.

If none of these options fit your rhythm, at the very least, use gift wrap and boxes made from recycled paper.

Green Steps

1. Green up your invitations, thank-you notes, and Christmas cards.

When you offer invitations or thank-you notes to your guests, can you do so electronically? This saves paper, time, and postage. Evite, Disney, Hallmark, and a variety of other sources offer online invitations. Have your child help to place a personal call to your guests without email. If you've just gotta send an invitation, consider sending it on seed paper. Several companies offer invitations printed on paper made of pressed seeds. Once the event is over, the recipient can toss the card into a dirt patch, water it, and up come wildflowers! Visit www.botanicalpaperworks.com or check out the Greenfield Paper Company at www.greenfieldpaper.com (they also offer cards made from junk mail and hemp).

Consider electronic Christmas cards. Many families send lovely letters to friends and family to catch them up on the events of their year. If you do this electronically, you can savvy the missive up quite a bit, add more graphics and photos, and save paper and postage in the process. With stamps now running at almost fifty cents, you can save some solid money here.

2. Reconsider how you serve your food.

Driving down the street in your neighborhood on trash day, you can easily spot who had a party last weekend. Extra bags filled with plates, cups, and flatware line the curb. Empty pizza boxes or giant containers from catering companies poke out of the trash cans. Avoid the curbside heap by purchasing reusable party ware that will last throughout the years. Catering? Order from a company that serves from reusable trays or pans that they later return to pick up, or cater from a company whose serving materials can easily be cleaned, reused, or recycled. If your favorite place does not offer any of these options, see if they will let you drop off your own platters and utensils to bake with and deliver to your home.

Serve pre-made drinks from pitchers and jugs. Try to avoid all the packaging of juice boxes, individual servings of milk, or water bottles. Offer little guests a swig of organic grape juice from an eco-friendly sippy cup or reusable water bottle they can take home at the end of the party.

3. Give Green.

Send kids home with goodie bags made from reused or recycled material. If you have the time, you can help your kids make and decorate bags from old fabric. Take a trip to a resale shop or your attic and grab some old curtains or sheets. With a few stitches (Martha Stewart is not looking) you can offer a reusable bag to fill with goodies. My friend Lauren keeps a box of trinkety toys (many of which her children received in goodie bags). It's a box filled with odds and ends her kids will not miss, and when she has a party, all the party guests get to create their own bag of treasures from this box. A great way to repurpose their potential trash into another child's treasure.

When you give a gift, give something green. Even your most discriminating friend can appreciate a durable reusable bag. Stainless steel bottles now come in an array of colors and designs. Organic cotton T-shirts make lovely presents, and soy-based candles offer fragrances without petroleum. Friends who may not make these choices on their own might consider using these items if you do the work of picking them out. Also, remember that giving to a charity in your friend's honor is a great way to educate.

Also, consider going more natural when it comes to seasonal decorations. I'm not convinced that we all need giant inflatable snow globes with a Santa Claus and Frosty in our front yards. Decorate with items you already have or pull the outside in. A few branches clipped from a pine tree with a handful of pine cones can make a lovely table display at Christmas. Seashells and even sand placed in the right container can make great decorations. For Easter I purchase a bright hydrangea plant as a centerpiece and then drop it into my backyard after the holiday. Gourds at Thanksgiving or patriotic flowers on the Fourth are all natural ways to decorate without adding to our landfills. Have your kids choose the foliage they want to use and then let them decorate with it. It makes great family fun and helps them understand their natural world.

4. Make your choice: real or artificial Christmas tree?

Every December this question becomes a hot topic on the green scene. The best choice is to visit a local tree farm to cut down your own tree; after that, it gets complicated. Tree farms plan on this business and replace the trees each year, so this is sustainable use. Local farms are close, so the gas required to get the tree home is minimal. Another option is to visit a local tree lot. However, these trees are trucked in from all over the country and are normally cut three to four weeks before you get it home. The fuel required to get the trees to your lot is significant, but many tree lots benefit charitable organizations, so here your money is well spent. You can also decorate with a potted Christmas tree and set it into the ground once the holiday is over (or once the ground thaws if you live in a colder climate). Keeping the tree alive and planting it properly may take a bit of gardening finesse, but this option adds a tree to the earth, and who can complain about that?

The last option is the artificial tree, which many people think is actually more green than it is because it does not require the chopping down of an actual living Douglas fir or blue spruce. But the tree is likely shipped in from overseas and probably manufactured with harmful chemicals. Then again, if you keep those plastic branches for twenty years, things start to even out when compared to the amount of fuel it takes to get two decades' worth of trees to your local lot.

5. If you do decide to mail Christmas cards (or birthday, etc.), send out cards that make a difference.

Our family sent cards from an organization called Chicago Lights one year. The cards were designed by children, the images represented the city where we live, and the proceeds went to an amazing ministry through Fourth Presbyterian Church in Chicago (www .fourthchurch.org/chicagolights.html). Similar card programs are available in other cities and through other charitable organizations.

If you flip the card over, most of these greetings will tell you what organization they sponsor and why they created the card. It can be a neat way to share a message beyond "happy birthday." Of course, look for cards printed on recycled paper as well.

6. Explore nontraditional gift registries.

The Center for a New American Dream offers an alternative gift registry, available for new babies, birthdays, and other events. This is an absolutely amazing way to ask for less and to offer your friends a cost-effective way to celebrate your family (quite timely, given the economic realities of our day). You can tailor the registry to include meal requests, used instead of new clothes, prayers for your child, babysitting, and links to eco-friendly products you would like for your event. Check it out at www.alternativegiftregistry.org.

Your Eco-Examen for Chapter 9

❑ What is one new tradition I would like to try this year?

❑ What is one idea from this chapter that does not work for my family?

10

Water Bottles and Jet Fuel:
Green on the Go

Spend the afternoon. You can't take it with you.
ANNIE DILLARD

Go slowly, there is such little time.
ADELE CALHOUN, *THE SPIRITUAL DISCIPLINES HANDBOOK*

My friend Liz is the greenest mom I know. She is committed to a greener way of life, not just to the trend as it pops up in our culture. She was green before it was cool to be green. She's an advocate for the earth and a gardener too. Liz provides earth-friendly and home remedy options to her family, they eat organic food, and even use a gas-free push mower at her house (not so much fun when it's 90 degrees in August). And she does it all without making me feel like a complete, not-green-enough loser.

Being the green mom that she is, the year hybrid cars hit the mainstream market, Liz and her family were among the first to get a hold of one. Riding in it felt a bit like cruising in a mini spaceship, sort of like Jane Jetson in a Toyota. It seemed to hover at stop lights, no shaking, rattling, or even the hum of an engine could be heard. Just silence and the glow of the computer console telling you exactly how much gas you were (or were not) using at that moment.

As my friend Liz enjoyed her new ride, I too began to picture myself as a hybrid owner, driving off into a green sunset of lower emission bliss. Then I turned around and took stock of the quaint little backseat. For someone like me, who treats her car as a second closet, I woke quite startled from my hybrid daydream.

I carry not one but two strollers in my car, along with three kids and their car seats, an old gym bag, two umbrellas, and flip-flops. Backpacks and art projects ride on top of the strollers. Most weeks I haul around two to three bags of old clothes for whichever friend needs 3T pants. Overdue library books have been known to take cover under the passenger seat, and I am fairly certain my husband has at least two flashlights and a screwdriver stashed in there. And on occasion, our six-foot-eight cousin Sam and our three-hundred-and fifty-pound friend Big Dave end up in our car.

The hybrid shift was looking grim.

But it matters how we get from here to there. So what does an eco-conscious family do when deciding how to travel?

My adventure in Liz's hybrid reminded me of the fact that we do not need to drive hybrids to think more greenly about how we get around (although if you can indeed make this switch, you should). Nor do you need to swap the minivan for an old Schwinn. Just by making a few simple travel tweaks, your family can give a big break to the planet.

From Convenience
to Contemplation

As with creating a green budget, being green on the go also begins with a shift in mind-set. We live in a culture that worships the god of convenience. Just watch thirty minutes of television and notice how many ads promise a speedy clean-up, a faster way to lose weight, or quicker banking.

This cultural icon of convenience has failed us. We live in a world with more time-saving devices than at any other era in history, yet more people than ever claim they feel constantly hurried and busy. Our national time crunch has lured us into a mind-set that says if we can just move fast enough, we really can do it all.

Contrast this with Moses' words in Psalm 90:12: "Teach us to number our days aright, that we may gain a heart of wisdom." Or Solomon's words, in Ecclesiastes 3, that remind us of how God has set eternity into our hearts. God has placed the vastness of eternity into our very souls, which technically means we have all the time in the world, and yet we are still in a hurry.

Being green on the go begins by providing ourselves the space to contemplate the impact our "convenient" lives make on the earth. Which means thinking through where we go, why we are going, and why we insist on getting there so quickly. The first step in getting there greenly is to ask whether we really need to get there at all. Reining in our travels can reduce fuel consumption and carbon emissions as well as the impact of consumerism when we decide not to take that trip to the store.

If we take the time to contemplate wise choices rather than racing straight for the most convenient option, we can make more fruitful choices. We might grow our own food rather than drive to the grocery, or we might shop locally rather than hit the biggest mall we know. We can more easily find the space to pause and notice God's creation instead of zipping past on the way to the next errand. Reflection before action encourages our families to live slower lives. Lives that may be just a touch more sane than the ones we live now.

Slowly planning where we go and why can make a significant difference for our families and the planet.

Life in the Fast Lane

Americans are eternally "on the go." However frantic we may be, though, our culture of convenience has many aspects that I love. On a rainy day, I can get coffee and cash without ever leaving my car. I can fill a prescription or pick up dinner by simply rolling down my window. And if you enroll in a school program that has curbside drop-off, you can launch your children into education without even leaving the car. However, these time-saving maneuvers have become so commonplace that many families now view them as the best, and at times the only, way to get things done.

For most American families, the family car is literally the driving force behind all of these comings and goings. Americans own more automobiles per capita than any other nation in the world, roughly 800 per 1,000 people.[1] Emissions tests aside, we dump millions of pounds of carbon emissions into the atmosphere as a result of our attachment to our cars. Sadly, we're responsible for approximately 25 percent of the world's carbon emissions, even though we have only 5 percent of the population.

According to the US Census Bureau, the average American spends about twenty-five minutes getting to work each day (one way, including multiple forms of commuting).[2] At first, twenty-five minutes one way may not seem all that bad, until the math starts to snowball on you. Round-trip, it's almost one hour a day, five hours a week, which is close to twenty hours a month. So each month, most people say adios to an entire day of their lives that they spent commuting.

Most moms who work at home with their kids spend even more time in the car than this. A school pickup followed by a baseball drop off can easily gobble an hour. Add a play date three towns over to the endless string of errands and an at-home mom is not really at home, she's spending her day in the car. So before jumping into the driver's seat, ask yourself these potentially life-changing questions:

First and foremost, have I chosen a green place to live? The answer to this question can vary according to your circumstances. For some that might mean forty acres in a rural area, or it might mean access to public transportation. For others that might mean easy access by foot, bike, or car to the prominent people and places in their lives.

Do I live close enough to the amenities I need or the places I frequently visit? It's no good building a green, LEED certified house if that means you have to drive thirty miles every day to work or school. Next time you move, look not only at the cost of the home or the quality of the school system, but also consider commute times, everyday amenities (such as grocery stores), and access to the places you go to most (whether that be a church, library, health club, or something else).

Once you've looked at where you live and the places you frequent, you can ask other questions. Do I really need to do this today, or can I do it another time as part of another errand? Can I walk or bike there instead? Who else can I bring with me (is there a neighbor who needs to grocery shop at the same store)? Can I combine this trip with another errand (is the post office next door to the library)? Am I shopping locally? Are all my errands as close to my home as possible? If not, can I tweak a few to save on gas? If we learn to spend less time in our cars, we can begin to ease the ecological burden our automobiles have created.

When our family moved into our current home, we made a commitment to live as close as possible to the downtown area in our community. This meant that we would need to rule out certain living options like a brand new home or one on the perfectly spacious lot. Homes near town are more pricey, so it meant adjusting our spending to make the shift. But we live within walking distance of almost every major part of our lives. From school to the grocery store to the library, bank, post-office, pediatrician, and train station. The pool is just two blocks away too. So if you catch me driving, I don't have much of an excuse (unless, of course, it is 20 degrees below zero in January; that happens in Chicago).

Star Wars Lunch Boxes

So, for a family to trade in convenience for a little contemplation, we should ask questions about where we go and how we get there, but we also need to look at why we go and what we drag along with us. This means discovering how to honestly simplify things.

Take for example the "convenience" of drive-through food. I have a little fetish for a morning bagel at a nearby drive-thru. It's a big national chain, nothing special, but I find their bagels a fabulous way to start my day. If I am not monitoring myself, I will drive two miles out of my way, several days a week for this bagel.

Once they slap together my sesame with plain cream cheese, it is wrapped in super thick crinkly paper and tossed into a completely unnecessary paper bag that is really only used to get the bagel across that two-foot chasm from the drive-thru window and into my car window. This wasted bag comes complete with a pile of napkins and a plastic knife I will not use.

To get my breakfast I've wasted gas, paper, and plastic. If I just had my bagel at home, the packaging (while still present) would have been much less, I would have saved on gas and emissions, and I would have used my own knife to spread the cream cheese. It would have been simple. Green on the go means limiting these so-called convenient options whenever we can.

Being green on the go also means we take a hard look at how we ship our kids out the door with their lunches. School cafeterias generate volumes of unnecessary waste. It's sort of ironic really. Just down the hall they are learning about the vastness of the Amazon, the intricacies of the rain forests, and the woes of climate change.

Then they march to the cafeteria for lunch and whip heaps of plastic wrap, drink boxes, brown bags, plastic cutlery, and paper napkins into the trash.

Consider packing your child a waste-free lunch. Think back to the days of Strawberry Shortcake and Star Wars lunch boxes. According to wastefreelunches.org, the average kid generates sixty-seven pounds of lunchroom waste in one school year (this is more than many of them weigh). Check out www.wastefreelunches.org for ideas on how to go waste free when packing a lunch, as well as for information on programs to help your entire school implement a waste-free lunch program.

Sending your kids, yourself, or your spouse off with reusable bags and drinking bottles, cloth napkins, and reusable sandwich containers cuts down significantly on waste. Granted, there is always the reality that these nondisposable items suddenly become disposable when accidentally tossed into the trash or left on the bus. But, again, the payoff here is worth the pain.

Making this shift normally will not require you to spend money or burn gas getting to the store to purchase these things either. Most families have everything they need for a waste-free lunch sitting in their cabinets already. Plastic containers, old dishtowels or fabrics that can become napkins, odd cutlery that will not be missed should it land at the bottom of a locker. This shift is a money saver. If you are short on reusable items or want to look at some of the innovations (for all ages) in this emerging eco-market, give the products at www.laptoplunches.com or www.nubiusorganics.com a look.

On a Jet Plane

When I was in middle school, our eighth grade class took a trip to Washington, DC. For my midwestern classmates and me, this little adventure would mean air travel, and, as it turned out, I had made it to the ripe old age of thirteen without ever having boarded a plane.

As we followed our chaperones through O'Hare International Airport, I couldn't have cared less about the adolescent drama that unfolded all around me (of course everyone had to decide who they would date while on this trip). The endless backpacks filled with junk food and three days off school were also of no interest to me. My single focus was to calm my "I'm too scared to fly" nerves and get on that plane.

After a few gummi bears and some attention from my friends, I managed to pull my overdramatic self together as we roared down the runway. Somewhere around thirty thousand feet, I finally relaxed and was able to breathe again. The girl next to me was reading *Tiger Beat*, so this also helped.

While I had to wait thirteen years to fly, all three of my children have been on a plane during their first year of life. The thought of them making it to their adolescent years without air travel seems difficult to imagine. Today, families and friends are scattered across the country, and it appears that every sport from cheerleading to soccer eventually requires a tournament in Florida. Air travel is more a part of life today than ever before.

In 2006, 691 million passengers boarded planes in the United States.[3] Because millions of Americans zip across the sky every day, air travel seems so normal, so ordinary. It is a fact of American life that people fly. No one throws a party because you flew to Minneapolis.

Commonplace as American air travel has become, the majority of people on this planet never have, and never will, board an airplane. Air travel is really a luxury few in this world can afford. Families living in extreme poverty are not likely to book a ticket to Fiji. The number of people who fly seems insignificant when compared to those who remain grounded. Only one in three people fly each year.

Yet the ecological impact of those of us who fly contributes heavily to climate change. Air travel is one of the most ecologically disastrous ways to get places. According to the World Watch Institute, one plane crossing the Atlantic Ocean uses 16,000 gallons of fuel, which is enough to power one automobile for fifty years. In 2005, passengers on commercial flights flew a total of 3.7 trillion miles, which was the equivalent of 4.8 million people flying to the moon and back.

Commercial air travel accounts for roughly 3 percent of the world's carbon emissions. But this figure does not include the enormous carbon footprint of the airline industry that powers up airports across the world and has massive corporate headquarters in major cities. Add to that the impact of manufacturing and maintaining airplanes, and air travel comes with a hefty carbon price tag.

Doesn't seem fair, does it? That someone in Colombia or L.A. who may never fly is negatively affected by my vacation plans.

So how can we travel smarter? The thought of driving across the country with a carload of kids will send some parents screaming into a wall. For others, a road trip across the country is an absolutely essential American rite of passage. Wherever you land on this spectrum, before you book a plane ticket, ask yourself if you can get there by car or train (FYI, trains release one-third of the emissions planes do).

Ask yourself if you really need to go on that trip and if so, can you drive instead?

Take public transportation to and from the airport, when available, and consider buying carbon offsets to make up for your air travel (see chapter 7). Travel with reusable drinking bottles and coffee mugs, fill them up on the boarding side of security, and you are able to travel without that plastic bottle. Avoid waste by bringing your own snacks, and pass on taking the drinks or napkins offered on the plane.

Vacation with Purpose

I remember my husband and I in our honeymoon bliss stepping off the gangplank of a giant cruise ship. We were on day three of our Caribbean tour and stopped on the island of Dominica, a stunning little paradise in the Eastern Caribbean with all the rich heritage Jimmy Buffet would approve of.

It was the sort of postcard moment I still cherish: azure water, lush foliage, the smell of sunscreen. But not long after we arrived in Dominica, I began to notice that the realities of life on the island were dramatically different than the all-you-can-eat chocolate buffet I'd enjoyed the previous night.

The people of Dominica were warm and acted happy that we were there (since we would likely spend money). But they had probably never seen the Lido Deck. And while we were mingling in the same sunshine, our big white boat was a bit more dashing than the housing on their island.

As we made our way through the crowds to find a taxi, my husband asked me if I felt weird. I was busy eyeing all the kitschy knickknacks lining the street and halfheartedly said, "No. Why, honey?" His response was basically this: It felt weird to him that a few moments ago this was a mellow island where people were living and struggling to make life work, and then all of a sudden this giant boat filled with overweight, picture-taking, straw-hat-wearing Americans pulls up and disgorges them into the quiet little streets to do some shopping.

It was unsettling to him that the money we spent on that cruise could have provided school uniforms or materials to build a school or church on that island. And while it was good to give their economy a boost with our purchasing power, the disparity between rich and poor was glaring at that moment. I began to look around. Behind the cab drivers vying for our attention were rundown homes and abandoned stores. The Caribbean colors I love so much were muted by the dust and dirt of their unpaved streets.

Women and men of this island were doing their best to barter and negotiate with pushy tourists who wanted the best deal and the cheapest fare to the beach. These tourists (with significantly deeper pockets than the cabbies) had been coached by the cruise ship concierge to work every angle for a deal. Some of the cruisers looked around bewildered, almost as if they expected Dominica to look sort of like the Four Seasons. It was obvious they were hoping for a more luxurious port of call.

It was an odd moment. From that time forward, while I loved the steel drums and a pineapple drink as much as the next gal, that cruise gave me an overwhelming sense of guilt.

When we consider greening up our vacations, it does not mean that we have to ditch the beach to plant trees or do trail restoration on Mount Hood. We do not have to skip Disney World or the family reunion, but we do need an awareness of where we are going and why.

I know a family from our church who can afford to take their family just about anywhere they may want for vacation, but they purposely choose to limit their options because they want to give their kids an accurate picture of reality, they want their children to understand the fact that millions of other people don't get to go on vacation. Definitely a family who vacations with purpose.

Many families across the world cannot and do not regularly vacation. Many who live in the places we visit work very hard to provide the tours and luxuries we enjoy on our visit, and will never enjoy this sort of pampering themselves.

Purposeful vacations take into account the social imprint of your vacation as well as the ecological practices of the places you visit. What good does it do to trash the very environment you are heading off to visit? For example, skiing at a resort that does not monitor its carbon emissions is unsettling. Their annual snowfall, the very commodity they are selling, could diminish with climate changes.

A cozy visit to a seaside restaurant may be lovely, but it is not helpful if the seafood we enjoy comes from overfished waters. The snorkeling tour boat that dropped anchor onto a fragile coral reef sort of defeats the purpose. You may get to find Nemo that day, but after hundreds of anchors kill the coral, your children will not.

So before you travel, ask yourself what the ecological and social cost of your visit on an area may be. Make it a point to not only relax in the luxuries of that place, but to visit the real place, not just the vacation face. Meet the people, try to understand their lives and their journeys, look for green opportunities everywhere you go. Be an educated traveler and make a difference when you can.

Ultimately, being green on the go is about so much more than a hybrid car.

Green Steps

1. Green up your hotel and resort stays.

If your travels involve a hotel stay, bring home the half-used bottles of resort shampoos and lotions you might normally leave behind. Finish them up, and then recycle the containers. Also, look for water-saving tips from your hotel. Many offer programs to conserve water by asking you to reuse your towels and bed linens the next day. A card placed in the room usually provides visitors with tips on how to participate.

2. Consider an eco-vacation, a mission project, or a conservation trip.

Your family can have the opportunity to do everything from cleaning up trails or helping create habitat for endangered wildlife to serving needy families around the world. Your local church or park district may offer trips and ecotourism vacations to destinations where you and your family can serve together. Many Christian ministries offer short-term mission opportunities for middle school, high school, and college students (Youthworks and Youth With A Mission [YWAM] are two places to start). A Rocha is another organization with a Christian understanding of the world that offers opportunities to preserve God's creation both at home in the US and abroad (www.arocha.org).

3. All kidding aside, consider a hybrid car; they make a difference.

The auto industry is responding to consumer demand and several cars now come in hybrid options. From SUVs to compact cars, shop hybrids if you need a new car. But remember this simple little fact. The smaller and slower the car, the better the fuel efficiency. A hybrid Toyota Prius will get better mileage than a hybrid Chevy Tahoe. A four-cylinder Ford Escort will get better mileage than a six-cylinder, tricked out Ford Mustang. Think small and slow rather than big or flashy.

Your Eco-Examen for Chapter 10

❑ What is one idea from this chapter I will implement with my family?

❑ What is one idea from this chapter I will decide to set aside?

Green Worship:
Can Your Church Go Green?

The growing possibility of our destroying ourselves and the world
with our own neglect and excess is very tragic and very real.

BILLY GRAHAM, *APPROACHING HOOFBEATS*

Therefore, I urge you, brothers and sisters,
in view of God's mercy, to offer your bodies as a living sacrifice,
holy and pleasing to God—this is true worship.

ROMANS 12:1 TNIV

On most Sundays my family bursts through the double doors of our
church just moments before or—who am I kidding?—after the service has started. The five of us are a flurry of activity. Diaper bags,
jackets, and a slow-moving toddler are trailing behind us. We've got
to drop the baby off in the nursery, get the other kids settled, and
grab our bulletins, all before someone sits in our regular pew, which
is up front and a little to the right. For us, Sundays are packed with
a few songs, beautiful friends, and Noah's Ark crafts oozing wet glue
all over the one pair of khakis my son owns.

I worship at a great church. They adore my kids, the staff are
savvy and wise, the people are passionate, and they serve sprinkle

donuts. Sure, it has issues, but on a Sunday morning when I am hug-
ging my mommy friends while my kids run in circles, it feels good.
It feels like home. There is always so much to do on a Sunday morning so taking even a nanosecond to think about whether or not my
church was green rarely happened. But after I began greening up my
life, I started to notice the mountain of ecological crimes we were
committing, all in the name of Jesus.

Styrofoam Cups

After the service, where we sing of God's splendor and the beauty of
his creation, we file out of the sanctuary and toss our multi-page bulletins into a big shifting pile. Maybe they get recycled. We continue
moving down to the fellowship halls, where we grab a Styrofoam cup
of coffee (not fair-trade) with individually packaged creamers and
sugar. Meanwhile, the kids clamor for those sprinkled donuts and
another Styrofoam cup filled with the same artificial pink lemonade
they've poured since 1980.

Downstairs the middle school students slam sixteen-ounce bottles of Mountain Dew before Sunday school and they toss it into
the trash when they are done. There is no recycling bin by the pop
machine. Around the corner from these students, the copy machine is
hot to the touch; it has been launching reams of adult Sunday school
material across the building since 7:00 a.m. Much of this paper ends
up in the trash. It's the same in all the offices.

Our church, while progressive in many ways, served up their
Sunday morning details in the same stunted, not-so-green fashion
as many churches across the US. Now, thanks to members of our
congregation passionate about a more sustainable life, we have begun
to reverse this trend. We are on a journey to change these realities,
and it is making a difference in our congregation and community.

My husband and I have worshiped in several places. At most

a Styrofoam cup is required for admission. A bulletin printed on paper is the norm, and church recycling programs are spotty at best. Lights are continuously on, and the air conditioning runs so cold in the summer that you need boots and a fleece to survive the worship hour. Turns out, the very buildings that were designed to proclaim the wonders of the God of the universe are some of the least green places in the country.

Despite this disregard for nature, most Christians are quick to take Sunday morning liberties with creation. J. Matthew Sleeth, in his book *Serve God, Save the Planet* (one of the very best books on God's green life), points out what a prominent role images from nature play in our worship services. Most churches that use projection software like Power Point will shine images of bright blue skies, snow-capped mountains, or swirling rivers onto their screens. These snapshots of creation serve as the backdrop for worship songs and Scripture reading. These images are fitting, as people do not normally find themselves moved to praise by an oil spill or deforested hillside.

So worshippers project the words of St. Francis — "Oh brother wind, air, clouds, and rain, by which all creatures ye sustain. Oh praise ye, Alleluia" — onto a screen with a pine forest background. And as the choir sings, parishioners sit flipping through paper bulletins with stomachs hankering for that afternoon's potluck complete with paper napkins and plastic tablecloths. No one is aware that we are destroying the real places that inspired these hymns and images.

Why does the church, the place where we come to worship and honor the Maker of heaven and earth, pay such little attention to the actual creation itself? It is an inconsistency that is, well, inconsistent with our faith. In his article "The God Who Can't Be Tamed," Philip Yancey challenges Christians to live as though they really believe God's creation points us to God.[1] We often miss this. Like so many things that God asks us to do, it is hard to truly live what God says. This is one place in particular that it seems easy to bypass God's call.

The Luxury of Green

The nearly universal response when asked why churches (as well as many nonprofit community centers, park districts, etc.) are not green is that to be green costs too much. When all the numbers of a budget fall into line, there never seems to be enough capital to make all the hoped-for changes and adaptations. As a staff member at my church, I've heard many an indignant conversation following a cut to the budget area someone was passionate about. Resources are limited.

A plan to green up the place *appears* to come with an impossible price tag that most nonprofit budgets in today's economic climate cannot afford (but remember the principles of chapter 3 here). Waste haulers may charge an additional fee to remove recyclables from the site. Recycling bins can be costly. Fair-trade coffees and teas can be more expensive to serve than their commercial counterparts. Paper cups with recyclable hot sleeves are significantly higher priced than Styrofoam, and forget the cost of purchasing actual reusable mugs (although parishioners' bringing their own mugs is a fabulous idea). Then there are other details like swapping out lighting fixtures for energy efficient versions, adjusting heating and cooling systems, and installing water-saving kitchen and bathroom fixtures or a gray water collection system. The price tag can easily escalate. Considering only the cost, a church can rarely justify such changes. But when we look at the long-term savings, a church will normally make up more than the difference. Almost every energy-saving change will make up the cost.

Paying for a greener church is just one part of the perceived "problem." Many in church leadership agree that a greener congregation lines up with God's Word, but they shudder at the process of educating congregants along these lines. It may mean sermons, Sunday school lessons, and perhaps a capital campaign to pay for ecological stewardship changes. There will undoubtedly be a prosaic group of people who question if a greener life is theologically supported anyway. They fear that it will lead to worship of the creation rather than the Creator, or they crab that green living is pointless since this whole world will cease at the end of time anyway. Some shudder at the politically charged angle of green living because, frankly, *green* is a historically liberal name tag and some Christians may struggle with this. Many are simply ruffled by the thought of changing their Sunday routine.

If cost and theology are not enough, the volunteer power required for a greener Sunday can be daunting. For most churches volunteers are at a premium, and making the most of their time and talents shows respect for these individuals. Sidestepping the waste generated by Styrofoam coffee cups by offering ceramic mugs instead would require a team of people to wash them. And someone needs to take the recycling out each week. Understandably, people object that they are short on volunteers for Sunday school and cannot send the few folks they do have off to the kitchen, leaving empty classrooms behind! An understandable point. Green is a luxury many churches fear they cannot afford.

The Real Luxury

But isn't the opportunity to bask in the glory of creation the real luxury? Isn't leaving a world with clean water and places to find faith in God through creation as important as sitting in a classroom with those kids?

I confess an inadequacy when it comes to nitty gritty details of financial matters. But I have learned enough to believe that there is room in both the budgets and hearts of our churches to pursue a greener Sunday morning. We have reached the point in human history when our very lives depend on it. Greening up the church is not a fad or some hippie luxury; it is good stewardship and it is our future. In Yancey's article he goes on to say that as we destroy the earth, we rob people of the opportunity to know God's splendor. Congregations that encourage and equip their members to share Jesus with others thwart their own efforts at evangelism by removing one of their most powerful tools, the "luxury" of creation.

Stewardship vs. Trend

Good stewardship is an issue all good churchgoers can agree with, at least in principle. Many people who step back from a green initiative for their church will rally to the cause of good stewardship. But this is really what being green is about, taking care of what we have been given. In my own church, the hearts and minds of many people were moved by the idea of stewardship long before they were moved by the emerging green trend. Trends are fleeting. Long-term lifestyle changes that invite us to be better stewards will never go out of style. Jesus was never purposefully wasteful.

Green Mamas at Church

As a Green Mama, you can have an impact on your Sunday morning. Church research consistently reports than more women serve in volunteer and lay positions in the church than men, and, while almost every church employs more male than female staff, it is the women who consistently show up in larger numbers to teach Sunday school, sing in the choir, prepare meals, offer prayer, and water the plants. The church is teeming with women who have their hands in hundreds of ministries and programs. They invest more time and energy into the many facets of church life than men. Which means that Green Mamas everywhere are uniquely poised to make the essential tweaks and changes that add up to a greener church.

Green Pastors

People often ask how they can bring this greener way of life to their churches as well as other community organizations. It is not easy, but it is well worth pursuing. I served on the staff of a national non-profit organization, where I took on the implementation of a green program. The entire process was completely dramatic, fraught with misunderstanding, tension, and a sense of relief once I moved on and everyone could just toss their pop cans into the trash again.

But, as I type these words, my own church is looking at wiser ways to worship. If you, like me, have a pile of kids, baseball games, and laundry to get to, knocking on your senior pastor's door to chat about strategies for recycling paper may seem more than a little silly.

But it's not.

I knocked on our senior pastor's door and was met with great enthusiasm. The day I broached the idea, I discovered that another friend in the congregation was also heading in this direction. Within a week we had a team of folks that included experts in energy, green building, and several LEED certified architects. Another mom emailed to let me know that she is trying to live greener in her family and wondered if she could help. By the end of the week, we had a green team.

Of course it is not always this idyllic and easy to rally the eco-troops. But finding people who care about this stuff and are yearning for the church to care as well may be surprisingly easy once you start asking around. You will find this especially with wise, stewardship-minded people who live simple lives. They may not choose to label themselves as "green," but you may find they live more earth-friendly lives than most.

As moms, we all know that our kids watch what we do. When they catch us shoving half a brownie into our mouth at 5:00 p.m., they are quick to point out that though we said, "no snacks before dinner," we didn't really mean it. They watch us and they learn from us, so when we step forward, in plain view of our kids, and point out that caring for God's creation matters for the church, they learn that it really does. Even if our efforts are met with sighs and groans or a sharp "no." Even if we find ourselves labeled as that wacky earth mom, it still matters that we tried because our kids see this and they learn, and while we may not succeed, hopefully they eventually will.

While most churches in the US are not very green, green living matters to a rapidly growing number of congregants. If their schools, businesses, and public spaces are increasingly green, they will come to expect and even demand this same noble behavior from their churches. I once presented this conversation to a seminar of several hundred church women. At the end, the most consistent response I received was "thank God someone inside Christianity is finally talking about this stuff!" This was followed with comments brimming with optimism and enthusiasm.

If everywhere we go green living is more accessible, then the inconsistencies of a church that claims what God created matters but lives as though the earth does not start to become embarrassing and obstructive. And really, we don't need more of that. People both inside and outside the church are clamoring for a greener life, a life of better stewardship.

Be encouraged!

Getting Started

Now, where to begin. There are two levels of action that I believe we can take when it comes to greening up our Sundays. First, the most sweeping changes will obviously come from a senior pastor

who believes that this way of living should be implemented throughout the church. A simple meeting with him or her can be the start
of a green journey for your church. It will probably mean further
conversations with committees, elders, trustees, and others in leadership, but peacefully bringing the topic to the folks in charge of the
place is the best start.

The first question you will likely receive is who will spear-
head these green efforts? To which you need to be prepared with
an answer. After making your leadership aware of your dreams of
green living and God's heart for this issue, you need a strategy for
how to bring forth a greener Sunday. You do not have to lead this
green committee (and you may not be asked to do so anyway), or
have every detail ironed out, but it will be helpful to show that you
have thought through the green life further than "hey, here's a good
idea." You may want to gather names and information on people who
share this vision and are prepared to bring about this reality for your
congregation.

This team will need to research local recycling options, reason-
able tweaks to lighting and energy use, carbon footprints, and common sense adaptations to resource and water use in your building.
They will need to learn about sustainability and be ready to offer
ideas and solutions that address piles of paper bulletins and disposable spoons. Simply saying "hey, we should print on recycled paper"
does not help much. Offering a list of post-consumer materials and
the cost of switching to these resources is more advantageous.

Most pastors are phenomenally busy caring for the people in your
congregation, and while we must expect that they will echo the value
of a greener life, we cannot assume that they have the time to make it
happen. Your help will serve your church well. And if this all sounds
like quite a bit of energy, it's because it is. You are not alone. In your
congregation are architects, engineers, HVAC professionals, electri-
cians, researchers, organizers, teachers, and a myriad of others who

can answer the sustainable questions that will crop up. Perhaps at this moment they do not consider themselves purveyors of God's green dream, but after a few thoughtful conversations with you, they will. Whether your congregation is less than 100 or over 5,000, you can collect people and move them toward action with thoughtful, deliberate conversations and by recruiting a wise team.

Second, if your efforts at organizing the eco-troops in your church are met with animosity, know that you can always be covertly green. You can be sure to consistently turn off lights in empty classrooms and restrooms; you can take home your paper and recycle it there. You can take home all the paper bulletins from your church and recycle them on your own. You can collect cans and bottles wherever appropriate. You can tote your own coffee mug to church, and park your bicycle or hybrid car in the front row of the parking lot if that suits you. Whenever possible, you can demonstrate the wisdom of a green life to those you worship with on a weekly basis. A greener Sunday is part of God's design for his people; with enough patience and persistence, it will catch on.

Seeing Green Everywhere

The principles above work well in other settings. Once you start seeing green, you begin to notice all the places in your community where a few earth-friendly tweaks can add up big for the planet. Today, many community focal points from school districts to libraries to police departments are starting to see that one of the ways they can serve the public is to make sustainable changes.

Look for this progress and see how you can help it along. If you live in a place where these eco-adaptations have been slow to come, sit down with community leaders and begin the conversation. This may mean going to your school board or the board of directors at your community centers and locating the people who make these decisions. Just as a greener life makes sense in the church, it makes sense that the organizations striving to nurture our kids, protect our families, and educate our children would see sustainable living as an indispensable partner for these goals. The same is true for local and national retailers and corporations.

All this may sound like a daunting task, and, really, it is. So let's be honest; if I walk into the closest Big Giant Super Mart and ask for the manager so that we can chat it up about carbon offsets, I know I will receive a strange look and will be placated by some warm-fuzzy answers. I know that the manager takes her lead from corporate executives twenty levels removed from her, and I will never meet them, let alone get an appointment to talk about the environment. Being a Green Mama does not necessarily mean that you have to stomp through the automatic doors and demand that all the light fixtures be swapped for LED lighting.

It can mean this, especially if you have a little Erin Brockovich in you, but for most of us it means sending the appropriate letters to your local government or getting involved in a national movement to become a bit greener. This may take the form of campaigning, financial support, or volunteer efforts in organizations aimed at ecological change. Looking for a God-oriented version? Check out A Rocha at www.arocha.org or the EEN (Evangelical Environmental Network).

If this level of activity feels a little too granola for you, continue to simply move more greenly through all the areas of your community. Encourage people to use your local library rather than buying books (yes, even this book). Be a champion for your local stores by nudging your friends and family toward shopping there. Ask your park district to offer a class on sustainable living, and be sure to recycle their brochure, or better yet, download it. Help your kids start an eco club at their school.

Tell the bagger at your grocery store that you do not need a separate bag for your gallon of milk. It sends me into a tailspin when someone bags my milk. It has a handle! Tell them to skip that bag, and then explain why. It will take you longer to check out than most people, and the sixteen-year-old boy trying to bag your milk does not want to hear about it, but tell him why you skip the bags anyway.

Talk up your green life whenever you can. Not pridefully, just commonsense-fully. If, as Paul tells us in Romans, our daily lives are an act of worship, then our daily activities should reflect this reality. Our Sundays should reflect this as well. Not just in hymns and pews, but in the coffee, paper, and ordinary moments that make up Sunday morning worship.

Green Steps

1. Learn from an eco-friendly church.

Take some tips and notes from places that are already green on Sunday mornings. Contact their staff and hear their story on how they went green; listen for the principles that will apply to your church. Keep an eye on an organization called Flourish (www.flourish conference.com). In 2009 they offered their first National Conference on Creation Care, a place for church staff and congregants to touch base on everything from greener facilities to Creation Care sermons.

Tri Robinson's book *Saving God's Green Earth* (Boise, Ida.: Ampelon, 2006) may also be a helpful resource. Robinson is the Senior Pastor of Vineyard Christian Fellowship in Boise, Idaho, a man who understands the call to both the senior pastorate of a vibrant church as well as the call to environmental stewardship.

2. Pick up a copy of the Green Bible.

If your pastor or church leadership needs a nudge, point them toward a copy of the *Green Bible* (San Francisco: HarperOne, 2008). This copy of the New Revised Standard Version highlights with green print all the places where Scripture talks about creation. Simply thumbing through the pages will reveal thousands of words that reveal our relationship with God through creation. The foreword by Archbishop Desmond Tutu and the essays from prominent voices like N. T. Wright, Pope John Paul II, and Barbara Brown Taylor will bend the ear of those hardest to convince. It is also printed with soy-based inks on recycled paper.

3. Explore the Evangelical Climate Initiative (www.christiansandclimate.org).

Encourage your senior pastor and church leadership to sign their "Climate Change: An Evangelical Call to Action" statement. This statement shows a commitment to work toward sustainability and change. It can also serve as a persuasive tool for you. If your pastor shrugs off this issue or is curious to know of prominent folks who care about these issues, let him or her know it has been signed by folks like Leith Anderson, Rob Bell, Luis Cortes, Andy Crouch, Timothy George, Bill Hybels, Ron Sider, and Rick Warren (a complete list of signatories is available on their website).

Your Eco-Examen for Chapter 11

☐ What is one green idea from this chapter that will work at your church?

☐ What is one green idea from this chapter that you would not implement at your church?

Plant a Tree:
Looking Out for Every Mom

What we call Man's power over Nature turns out
to be a power exercised by some men
over other men with Nature as its instrument.
C. S. LEWIS

When you harvest your land, don't harvest right up
to the edges of your field or gather the gleanings from the
harvest. Don't strip your vineyard bare or go back and pick up
the fallen grapes. Leave them for the poor and the foreigner.
LEVITICUS 19:10 MSG

How many computers, phones, televisions, or video game systems have you had in your lifetime? I remember the Apple IIe computers on which we played *Oregon Trail* when I was in junior high. The screen was black except for a green blinking cursor and letters. Today these computers have disappeared, replaced by laptops, touch screens, SMART boards, and other educational technology.

The year I met my husband, he had a car phone in his Oldsmobile Cutlass. An actual car phone—the base was mounted to the center console. To take the phone with you meant carrying a book-sized leather case complete with an antenna. My first mobile phone felt like it weighed five pounds, and it would not fit into any pocket of my jeans. In college, surfing the internet was not possible from the dorm and using email was a cutting-edge hobby reserved for computer science majors.

Today I use my phone to check email at stoplights. I get a new laptop every few years. Almost everyone on the treadmills at the gym has an iPod, and interactive gaming systems like the Wii have replaced the one-red-button joysticks of the Atari days. Have you ever wondered what happened to your last phone, that old television from your first apartment, or your old Sony Walkman once you dropped it into the trash or even the recycling bin?

Technology Comes to Ghana

In Ghana, West Africa, in the town of Koforidua, sits an electronics recycling site. Here, used electronics from the US, Europe, and other parts of the world come to be refurbished or recycled. Here, according to Greenpeace, open fires and piles of melting metal and plastic release high levels of toxic lead, chlorinated dioxins, and other known carcinogens into the soil and local drinking water. Here, children as young as age five work to break down, separate, burn, and organize used televisions, computer monitors, and other electronic waste. Here containers and shipments of e-waste that can be traced back to Korea, the Netherlands, Germany, and the United States form toxic heaps for the people of Ghana to sort and redistribute on our behalf.[1] This is how many of our electronics are recycled today: They are sent here.

In Western China children live near e-waste dumps. In India electronic waste is burned and sorted by children who have been found to have high levels of lead in their blood streams. And this despite the fact that India banned the import of electronic waste in 1997.[2] Most of it is imported today under the guise of charitable donations, even though they are not really used for anything other than scrap. Children often work the waste dumps looking for copper and other useful materials. To find them they burn the plastic covers to reveal copper wiring that can be sold.

Greenpeace International offers an in-depth exposé on the electronic waste recycling in Ghana (www.greenpeace.org), but simply look up "electronic waste and the poor" on your internet browser and you will find images that can haunt you. Barefoot ten-year-olds running through smoldering piles of plastic, wearing dirty soccer jerseys or clothing that advertises American companies. Little children, faces blackened with poisonous ash, carrying keyboards and television screens.

I Thought I Recycled It

When I pitch a glass bottle into our blue recycling bin, I am 99.9 percent sure it will be recycled. Sure, I have my doubts when the recycling truck that looks almost as greasy and slippery as the garbage truck comes wheeling down our street and a strong, hurried guy hops out and tosses my attempts to save the planet into the side of his truck. My glass mixes with plastic and paper and the pickle juice that my neighbor forgot to rinse out of her glass jar. Pizza boxes wrestle with cereal boxes as the truck screeches around the corner and out of sight. I watch it go and hope that somehow my plastic milk jugs become playground equipment or deck furniture.

Electronics recycling is a different game. When electronic waste ends up tossed into our landfills, it adds noxious chemicals like cadmium to the leachate that eventually creeps out of the landfill and into our soil and water. Knowing this, many thoughtful folks have decided wisely to recycle it, but these recycling programs often end up dumping "donations" of outdated computers onto barges, where they are shipped into the hands of children who need money for their families.

Our insatiable appetite for new technology paired with companies that refuse to offer smart disposal programs can mean that your computer recycling program is poisoning children who work the dumps in India. And while we ship our old cell phones across the ocean, closer to home we dump our trash on the poor every day. How many wealthy communities do you know with a landfill in their backyard? In the United States roughly 85 percent of all toxic land-fills are in lower income minority neighborhoods.[3] Superfund sites (places where hazardous waste is uncontrolled and likely infecting the surrounding area) disproportionately end up in impoverished areas.

The poor are less likely to receive the advocacy, education, and healthcare that it takes to fight the large corporations, waste man-agement companies, and governments that allow the waste from my last shopping spree to infiltrate their backyards and playgrounds.

Environmental Injustice

The dump-and-run philosophy that our culture supports, albeit unconsciously, serves up a hearty dish of environmental injustice that prevents another mom from giving God's best to her children. Like all moms, I want the very best this life can offer for my children. But unlike most moms in this world, I can actually come pretty close to giving my kids what American culture deems the best.

My children attend strong schools and sign up for sports leagues. These schools are nowhere near a landfill, and, thanks to the EPA, the air quality on and off the soccer field is mostly regulated. When my children come home, an icy fridge filled with fresh produce and organic milk awaits. They've never pillaged the trash looking for precious metals, and if I told them to burn a pile of wiring and pull out the copper, they would think I'd gone mad. Yet my lifestyle can push another family to the edge of the dump.

God's desire that we care for his creation is a call to action for more than saving old growth forests or coral reefs; it is ultimately a call to help people. We are the crown of God's creation, and the whole world of green living is inextricably linked to caring for one another. When we pursue an insatiable lifestyle, it damages the people who make our goods, ship our goods, and then remove them through our trash. When we pursue a less-than-green lifestyle, we damage our own attempts to truly know that we have enough, that gaining the whole world, yet forfeiting our souls (see Mark 8:36) happens every day in a billion little ways.

I cannot imagine what it must feel like for a fifteen-year-old in Ghana to rip open a box of useless computer cables that were donated to his trash heap. He sorts through them and realizes that he will need to melt all the wrapping off to get to the copper so that he can bring a few bucks home to his family. So he dumps the box over and lights the fire, watching as the cloud of toxins darkens his face and lungs. This is the best option he has to help his family.

Think about this: the people who sent over this toxic box also claim to be the most Christian nation on the planet. But what sort of Jesus would let children suck down carcinogens every day so that others can celebrate Christmas by giving new gadgets? If we say we love Jesus, then we must love his planet, and our brothers and sisters with whom we share this world.

It is impossible to lavish the fullest expression of God's love to other people without caring for his creation. To care for God's people is to care for the earth. The two are inseparable.

That Escape Plan

As a mom raising a family in our post 9/11 world, I have had panicky nights when I contemplate the horrors that might destroy our country: perhaps a nuclear holocaust, biological warfare, or some sort of terrorist attack. As these thoughts flicker through my mind, I try to reassure myself that someone would come to our rescue if my world ever imploded. I reason that surely the UN would step in if I ever found myself on the run in a war zone, smack in the middle of a famine, unable to find clean water, or raising sick kids in a trash heap. Maybe our allies would send in thousands of troops to whisk us away to safety?

I'm quite foolish and naive.

As I ponder these possibilities from my warm bed, complete with flannel sheets and a snoring husband, my mind tumbles into a horrific, desolate place. Perched firmly atop my little world of safety and security, these are times when I dare to craft that "what if" mental list many of us make when our imaginations get trapped in the darkness. My list goes something like this: If we were ever attacked, I would have to rush out to the garage and grab all our camping gear so we could survive. I would have to pack backpacks and make do without sippy cups and diapers. I try to recall how much gas is in the car and how far we could get before it ran out. Then I remember that I am always on empty and I contemplate sneaking out to fill up at that very moment. Just in case. But it is 2:00 a.m. and I do need some sleep.

I imagine myself fending off murderers, hiding my children in closets, and praying that they will not cry while marauders search our house. *The Diary of Anne Frank* still haunts me. I think about how hard it would be to leave my scrapbooks and their keepsake boxes behind.

By morning I am depressed and can hardly rally myself for coffee, let alone cartoons on PBS. I devote most of my mental energy that next day to wondering who will save us. I am an American, I am eternally optimistic, and I like to think the rest of the world owes me one, so "who will save us?" seems like a legitimate question.

As my imagination continues its nosedive, I remember that millions of moms around the world ask this very question each day.

There are the stories of civil war in the Congo. Mothers in poverty watch their daughters sold to the sex trade in India. In the Sudan tribal conflicts pit families against one another and mothers literally watch their children die before they themselves are beaten or killed. In Cairo mothers and children live together in the dumps. They do not fret over keepsake boxes.

I once saw a picture on the Mars Hill Bible Church website. A woman in Zambia working as a seamstress sat behind a sewing machine with a newborn on her lap. It was not take-your-daughter-to-work day. Other moms spend their days walking miles for anti retroviral drugs to manage their own HIV/AIDS diagnosis or their infected children, only to be told to come back tomorrow. Still others say farewell to a child who just died of malaria (a perfectly preventable disease).

I once served on a mission team in the Dominican Republic. We helped build a school for children who did not have one. The neighborhood was buzzing about the arrival of sixteen American high school students and the two of us adult leaders. After a week of building and playing soccer, singing and hanging out in the barrio, we had a farewell dinner with our new Dominican friends. During the dinner I sat on the floor holding a one-year-old child on my lap. His mother was single and dirt poor. I snuggled her child and cooed at him.

Later that evening the mother of that child and a local who spoke English came up to me. They asked me if I would take her son home to the US and raise him. I was barely twenty-four years old at the time. I cried. She cried. She wanted him out of poverty. Out of the dirt and the hunger and the illness. I wanted him out too.

These are the sort of situations mothers around the world are in constantly. They must decide life and death situations for their children each day. At times they must decide which child will get medicine and care and which must go without it; sometimes there is just not enough for everyone. All the while I decide whether or not we have time to hit Target before dinner. So I then ask myself, as I ponder my own escape plan, if I could be part of the escape plan that these moms are waiting for?

Am I part of the plan?

This is a painful question, mostly because I think the answer is yes.

The escape plan looks something like this. I start seriously considering what is truly important in my life. I limit what I own and need and want. I make educated decisions on what I buy and who I buy it from. I take the time to invest in renewable energy sources, limit my water use, turn off a few lights, and get some canvas bags. I teach my children that wrapping paper is not from the North Pole, and I take them outside on Christmas Eve to find a star. I teach them that Jesus loves them not for what they have but for who they are. I pray as often as I can about the harsh realities of this world. I might dabble a bit in carbon offsets and drive to San Diego for spring break instead of flying or I might decide to skip spring break altogether and donate the money to Compassion International. I pray some more and start to learn about the wider world and what others face on a daily basis. And I find a place that will recycle my old computers without sending them to dumps in India.

Becoming a Green Mama means we live in the way that honors God and other moms. In 2004, Wangari Maathai won the Nobel Peace Prize. Wangari is a Kenyan activist whose attempts to end deforestation have expanded to include the pursuit of social and justice issues. She cites environmental injustice as the root cause of most wars, because people tend to fight over limited resources. When asked by the National Geographic Live! speaker series what one thing we could do to help the world, she responded by simply telling the audience to plant a tree. Why? Because, according to Wangari, a tree is something we all can manage. Maybe we cannot battle negligent corporations, stop flying or driving places, or even define biodegradable, but in Wangari's words, "A tree is a very simple thing. Everybody understands a tree—just dig a hole, and water the tree and protect it from its enemies. Everybody can feel empowered."[4]

So Green Mamas, be empowered. God is behind you and in front of you, and what is left of his glorious creation is all around you. Hug your kids, hug your friends, hug a tree; and you will help another mom across the world to do the same. This is to live wisely and well.

Green Steps

1. Plant a tree.

Go plant something green. Whether you live in a high rise, on a farm, or anywhere in between. Plant basil in a window pot or a sugar maple in your yard. Plunge your hands into the dirt and bring forth life. As you till your patch of earth, remember the mothers around the world who need hope and healing on their own patch of earth. After you plant on your own, consider regular contributions to an organization that helps plant trees where they are needed most.

The Arbor Day Foundation (www.arborday.org)
American Forests (www.americanforests.org)
Floresta (www.floresta.org)

2. Find responsible recyclers.

When it comes to electronics, we need to take the extra step to be certain that the products you are turning in to be refurbished or recycled are indeed handled in a safe manner. Companies like HP offer electronic recycling programs with integrity. Before you send it in or trade it in, ask where it eventually ends up.

3. Pray.

As a mother it catches my breath each time I hear of another mom who must watch her children struggle. I can barely handle the reality that my children must survive the drama of middle school, let alone deal with something far more significant like disease or even death. But moms around the world lose children every minute of every day. Every single minute. At the very least, I owe them my prayers, my honest, committed, gut-wrenching prayers. Only a mother's heart knows the ache that groans in the very soul of a woman who must watch her child suffer. And when that suffering is unnecessary, or worse, somehow heightened because of our careless decisions, the agony is unbearable. This moves me to my knees. I pray it moves you to kneel and intercede as well. At the very least, we must pray. Pray for peace. Pray for wisdom. Pray for strength. Pray for change. Pray for hope. Pray for healing. Pray that we can empower and encourage. Pray that we can make a positive impact in this world.

Jana's Perfect Planet Play Date

My friend Jana is probably the most creative mom I know. Here is a play date that she once hosted for our kids. A great way to help elementary school age children and toddlers understand the places and people God's planet holds.

You will need a globe, broken green and blue crayons, an old paper coffee cup, coloring pages of a globe/earth. You will also need to check the book *Can You Say Peace?* by Karen Katz out of your local library.

Take the old paper coffee cup (from the time you forgot your reusable mug) and after rinsing it out, trim it down to about two to three inches tall. Then take broken bits of blue and green crayon that you normally would throw out and place them into the cup. Put them on a cookie tray and place them into the oven at about 200 degrees for eight to ten minutes. Once melted, take them out to cool.

While they are cooling, read the book *Can You Say Peace?* to the children. This book teaches them how to say "peace" in different languages. Have them find the various countries on the globe. After this you can check the melted crayons. Once they have cooled, unwrap the paper cup and you will have a circle crayon that looks like the earth. Have the children color their planet coloring pages with their new earth crayon. Discuss how wonderful it is to reuse broken things like crayons and turn them into something useful. You can also discuss with them how doing this helps all the people in the world, like the ones you just read about.

And if you are super fabulous like my friend Jana, you can top off the day with an organic sugar cookie iced to look like the earth.

So When Did You Get Into That?

I shared a tense meal once with a mom I barely knew. As we made the appropriate small talk, she served her sons lunch off paper plates wrapped in aluminum foil. I watched this and cringed as if I were biting on that foil. When I told her about my green life, in an irritating, peppy little voice she quipped, "Oh, so how long have you been into that?" As if it were a hobby like collecting stamps or ceramic poodle figurines.

My first instinct was to unleash upon her all I knew about God and the planet and the waste management industry that would end up hauling her perfectly reusable foil off to a landfill. If I am honest, I will tell you that I wanted to slap her silly because she talked a lot about God but did not seem to know a bit about caring for his creation. But I showed restraint; there was no showdown.

The more you learn about the green life, the more you will notice the millions of eco-crimes people commit as they destroy our children's world. You will find yourself fuming over formerly benign things like sandwich baggies, and you will shudder when offered a bottle of water. But show grace and practice patience. Every mom must make this journey on her own, and if you pout about her chocolate choices or aluminum foil, she will not want to learn from you how to make a better decision. Be strong but be gracious.

It is also possible to obsess over your new green life. What if your chocolate is organic but not fair-trade? What if your local farmer sells corn at the farmer's market but it was not grown organically? I've actually sat in the parking lot of my grocery store after forgetting my reusable bags and tried to calculate what would be better for the planet: to waste gas by going home to get them or to save that gas and haul everything home in plastic. Do what you can. It is not a black and white world; it is green. Don't make yourself crazy.

Finally, remember our job as parents is to pass along the wisdom of God to our children. Psalm 78:4 says:

> *We will tell the next generation*
> *the praiseworthy deeds of the Lord,*
> *his power, and the wonders he has done.*

As moms we are invited to tell our children about God's wonders, and one of the biggies is this planet. When it comes to passing on lessons about God, we all know the power of words can fail. Sometimes we just need to step outside and soak up the beauty of the earth. Sometimes the best way to tell of God's love and power is to stretch out with your sons and daughters on the warm earth and pull the sunshine into your souls. And if we want to make this wonder and warmth real for the next generation, we need to start living as greener, wiser mamas today, or they will live an impossible tomorrow.

The Green Mama
Resource Guide

Organizations to Consider

A Rocha (www.arocha.org): A Christian conservation organization active in eighteen different countries (and growing)

Blessed Earth (www.blessedearth.org): Organization created by the Sleeth family; offers great downloads, resources, and thought-provoking material on creation care issues

Center for a New American Dream (www.newdream.org): Organization aimed at curbing consumerism and helping people live more thoughtful, balanced lives

Compassion International (www.compassion.com): Child sponsorship programs

Environmental Defense Fund (www.edf.org)

Evangelical Climate Initiative (www.christiansandclimate.org)

Flourish Creation Care (www. flourishonline.org)

Heifer International (www.heifer.org): International organization that promotes strong communities, social justice, sustainable agriculture and policy change around the world

Target Earth (www.targetearth.org): Christians serving the poor and
   the planet in fifteen countries

Sierra Club (www.sierraclub.org)

World Vision (www.worldvision.org): Christian organization aimed
   at promoting social justice and ending poverty; also offers a child
   sponsorship program

World Wildlife Fund (www.worldwildlifefund.org)

Books for Kids and Teens

The Gift of Nothing by Patrick McDonnell (New York: Little, Brown,
   2005). For all ages; an illustrated, thoughtful, yet whimsical look at
   material goods versus the presence of people you love.

*I Love Dirt: 52 Activities to Help You and Your Kids Discover the Wonders
   of Nature* by Jennifer Ward (Boston: Trumpeter Books, 2008). A
   pocket guide with a simple activity for every season and week of the
   year.

*It's Not Easy Being Green: One Student's Guide to Serving God and
   Saving the Planet* by Emma Sleeth (Grand Rapids: Zondervan,
   2008). For junior high and high school students.

My Bag and Me! by Karen Farmer (New York: Penton Media, 2008).
   For ages two to six; comes with a reusable bag; the story of a child
   who brings a reusable bag to the store and learns how to make a
   difference this way.

My Space, Our Planet: Change Is Possible organized by Jeca Taudte
   with submissions for planet friendly living from the MySpace
   community (New York: HarperCollins, 2008). Great if you have or
   know of a teen who lives in the MySpace world.

Ten Things I Can Do to Help My World by Melanie Walsh (New York:
   Walker Books, 2008). Fun and easy eco-tips for kids; colorful,
   whimsical book made from 100 percent recycled material.

Books for Parents and Friends

Big Green Purse: Using Your Spending Power to Create a Cleaner, Greener World by Diane MacEachern (New York: Penguin, 2008). Another wonderful resource guide to point you toward everything from how to define ecological terms to how to eat local food and make fair and green consumer choices.

Common Wealth: Economics for a Crowded Planet by Jeffrey Sachs (New York: Penguin, 2008). Powerful information on poverty, economics, climate change, etc.; suggestions on how our crowded planet must do life differently if we want to survive; a great resource for those who want detailed information on sustainable living and why it matters.

The Complete Tightwad Gazette: Promoting Thrift as a Viable Alternative Lifestyle by Amy Dacyczyn (New York: Villard Books, 1998). Modest, sustainable, affordable options for living.

Cradle to Cradle: Remaking the Way We Make Things by William McDonough and Michael Braungart (New York: North Point Press, 2002). A thought-provoking look at the way we make things, challenging us to consider designing products that will nourish and nurture other products rather than our current manufacturing models.

Creation Care Magazine (www.creationcare.org). An extension of the Evangelical Environmental Network.

Everyday Justice: The Global Impact of Our Daily Choices by Julie Clawson (Downers Grove: InterVarsity, 2009).

Green, Greener, Greenest: A Practical Guide to Making Eco-Smart Choices a Part of Your Life by Lori Bongiorno (New York: Penguin, 2008). Filled with tips and tricks for eco-friendly living; each idea comes in three shades of green, allowing you to choose how deeply you want to dive into an option.

Rich Christians in an Age of Hunger: Moving from Affluence to Generosity by Ronald J. Sider (Nashville: Thomas Nelson, 2005). A timeless resource that raises tough but necessary questions about affluence and following Jesus.

Serve God, Save the Planet by J. Matthew Sleeth (White River Junction, Vt.: Chelsea Green, 2006). An outstanding overview of the green conversation inside and outside of Christian circles; includes helpful hints on how to live greenly.

You Are Here: Exposing the Vital Link Between What We Do and What That Does to Our Planet by Thomas M. Kostigen (New York: HarperOne, 2008).

Gardening, Composting, and Local Food

Animal, Vegetable, Miracle: A Year of Food Life by Barbara Kingsolver, Steven L. Hopp, and Camille Kingsolver (New York: HarperCollins, 2007).

Go Native!: Gardening with Native Plants and Wildflowers in the Lower Midwest by Carolyn A. Harstad (Bloomington, Ind.: Indiana University Press, 1999). For those of you in the Midwest, this one is a surefire winner.

In Defense of Food: An Eater's Manifesto by Michael Pollan (New York: Penguin, 2008). An eye-opening look at the hard truth behind what the average American eats and how to change our habits.

Natural Resources Conservation Service (NRCS) (www.nrcs.usda.gov). A department of the USDA that offers tips and how-to information for backyard composting—just type "composting" into the home site search feature.

Organic Gardening Magazine (www.organicgardening.com).

Worms Eat My Garbage: How to Set Up and Maintain a Worm Composting System by Mary Appelhof (Kalamazoo, Mich.: Flower Press, 1997).

Clothing

Happy Green Baby (www.happygreenbaby.com) offers a variety of children's clothing from several earth-friendly options like soybean fiber, bamboo, organic cotton, and merino wool. They are good for your baby and good for the planet, and they define their terms and offer an extensive list of what their products are made from. This is a label-reading dream come true. Just click on their Guide to Eco-Friendly Fabrics link for details; You will have a chance to learn what their fibers are, where they come from, and why they help.

Happy Green Bee (www.happygreenbee.com) offers comfy clothing for babies and children. Their unique twist is to offer a wide variety of gender neutral clothing that makes both boys and girls look adorable. This way kids can swap or pass down used clothing regardless of gender.

Kate Quinn Organics (www.katequinnorganics.com) lists adorable clothing for babies, kids, and even mamas too. They also offer bedding, bath, and body items.

Patagonia (www.patagonia.com) is a hallmark company for both mountaineers and everyday folks. Their products are manufactured with organic and eco-friendly materials, and the company itself has an impressive ecological track record.

Recycle Me (www.recyclemeorganictees.com) offers T-shirts made from 100 percent organic cotton grown and hand sewn in the US.

Tom's Shoes (www.tomsshoes.com) will give a pair of shoes to a child in need when you buy a pair. Their pink camo Tiny Toms are my favorite, but they've got tons to choose from (for moms and dads too).

Other Goods for Babies and Children

Clif Kid Z Bars (www.clifbar.com) are fabulous on-the-go snacks for kids: organic, chock-full of vitamins, and from a company with eco-integrity.

Eco Child's Play (www.ecochildsplay.com) is an extensive website offering tips, ideas, and information on raising children in nontoxic, healthy homes. This is one of the best sites you will find on the green conversation as it applies to families.

Klean Kanteen (www.kleankanteen.com) is our favorite reusable bottle company. Klean Kanteens come in a variety of shapes, colors, and sizes. They also offer several bottle tops, including one that fits with an Avent baby bottle nipple. All are stainless steel, BPA free, and earth friendly.

Kushtush Organics (www.kushtushorganics.com) offers a wide range of bedding for children, from pillows to crib bumpers (as well as bath towels and even hemp shower curtains). They offer certified organic products that are made in the USA whenever possible (woo hoo!).

North Star Toys (www.northstartoys.com) is a company offering simple wooden pull toys, boats, and other classics from sustainably harvested forests. In addition, they recycle and donate their scraps.

Plan Toys (www.plantoys.com) offers green toys that are made with recycled or sustainably harvested materials. Their banjo is my middle son's favorite; their 4X4 Adventure Car is also quite fun.

Sprig Toys (www.sprigtoys.com) offers battery-free toys that still race and light up. Your kids are the power behind these toys, and having them power their own toys naturally avoids the tons of batteries we toss out each year. They move your kids from passive to active play, and they are eco-friendly and award-winning toys too! Their Eco-Trucks are the favorite gift in our house.

Personal Care Items

Burt's Bees (www.burtsbees.com) offers a Baby Bee Bubble Bath that is the foamiest earth-friendly bubble bath we've used. Lots of bubbles and good for the earth. Their Baby Bee Shampoo and Wash is also wonderful and gentle for little (and big) bodies.

Dr. Bronner's Soaps (www.drbronner.com) offers a fair-trade peppermint organic bar soap that will make you giddy in the shower or bath. It's minty, fresh, and everyone in our house just loves the way it feels. A clean wash with a conscience.

Pangea Organics (www.pangeaorganics.com) is an organic line of skin-care products made in Colorado. Their products get high marks on the Environmental Working Group's Skin Deep Cosmetics Safety Database and their bar soaps smell absolutely phenomenal.

Tom's of Maine products (www.tomsofmaine.com) are a staple in our home, in particular, their Silly Strawberry Fluoride-Free Toothpaste for kids. And for mom and dad, their Natural Cleansing Mouthwash (alcohol and saccharin free) tops off your dental care routine without the harsh sting and chemicals from other mouthwashes. Note: Tom's of Maine was recently purchased by the Colgate Company, so watch for product changes.

Fair-Trade Organizations and Products

Coffee Ambassador (www.coffeeambassador.com): Small organization that has developed a holistic approach to coffee by meeting the social, economic, and spiritual needs of their growers.

Equal Exchange (www.equalexchange.coop): One of the most established and trusted names in fairly traded goods, offering everything from coffee and tea to chocolates and healthy snack food.

Fair Trade Federation (www.fairtradefederation.org): An association of wholesalers and retailers who are committed to the principles behind fairly traded goods and products. Many smaller organizations offer products through this larger umbrella organization.

Far Flung (www.farflung.co.za): A nonprofit based in South Africa that empowers and trains female artists to focus their creative energy into making and selling goods to support their families.

Good African Coffee (www.goodafrican.com)

Kiva (www.kiva.org): An organization that allows you to directly loan money to small businesses around the world for as little as $25.

Transfair USA (www.transfairusa.org): Nonprofit, third-party certifier of fair-trade products in the US. Helps farmers and local communities compete in the global market.

World Fair Trade Organization (www.wfto.com)

World of Good (www.worldofgood.com): One of the largest vendors of fairly traded products. Their website boasts over 15,000 products that empower their producers.

Notes

INTRODUCTION: Why I'm a Green Mama

1. Barbara Kingsolver with Steven L. Hopp and Camille Kingsolver, *Animal, Vegetable, Miracle* (New York: HarperCollins, 2007). Disc 3, chapter 4 (compact disc).

CHAPTER 1: Wisely and Well: Teach Us How to Live

1. Elizabeth Royte, interview by Ira Flatow, *Science Talk*, NPR, July 4, 2008.

2. *The Container Recycling Institute*, www.container-recycling.org/mediafold/newsarticles/plastic/2006/5-WMW-DownDrain.htm.

3. Chris Borris, "The Hidden Life of Laundry," *Sierra*, September/October 2002. www.sierraclub.org/sierra/200209/hidden.asp.

4. Dennis Linn, Sheila Fabricant Linn, and Matthew Linn, *Sleeping with Bread: Holding What Gives You Life* (Mahwah, N.J.: Paulist Press, 1995), 6.

CHAPTER 2: Your One Big Thing: Think Big, Start Small

1. *World Wildlife Fund*, www.worldwildlifefund.org/species/finder/northern whiterhinocerous.html.

2. Todd Hartman, "Deaths of Trees 'Catastrophic,'" *The Rocky Mountain News*, January 15, 2008, http://m.rockymountainnews.com/news/2008/Jan/15/beetle-infestation-get-much-worse/.

3. Statement to the US House of Representatives by the Rocky Mountain Research Station, www.nwc.cog.co.us/docs/cbbc/rick_cables_USFS_testimony_061609.pdf.

4. Michelle Nijhuis, "Global Warming's Unlikely Harbingers," *High Country News*, July 19, 2004, www.hcn.org/issues/278/14853.

5. www.colorado.edu/admin/announcement_files/2204-uploaded/announcement-2204-6666.pdf. Pages 55–56.

CHAPTER 3: Eco-Snobs: How Much Will This Cost Me?

1. National Center for Health Statistics, "Asthma Prevalence, Health Care Use and Mortality, 2003–2005," www.cdc.gov/nchs/products/pubs/pubd/hestats/ashtma03-05/asthma03-05.htm.

2. National Institutes of Health: National Heart, Lung and Blood Institute, Data Fact Sheet: Asthma Statistics, 1–2; www.nhlbi.nih.gov/health/prof/lung/asthma/asthstat.pdf.

3. Coeli Carr, "String Theory," *Time*, 2007, www.time.com/time/specials/2007/article/0;28804,1706699_1707550_1823981,00.html.

CHAPTER 4: Too Much Stuff: Curbing Our Consumption

1. Elizabeth Royte, *Garbage Land: On the Secret Trail of Trash* (New York: Little, Brown and Co., 2005).

2. Court Pearman, "Resource Consumption: U.S. vs. China," *Epoch Times*, February 12, 2007, www.theepochtimes.com/jiuping/newsletter/issue89/#6.

3. The Center for a New American Dream, *Tips for Parenting in a Commercial Culture*, April 2006, www.newdream.org/kids/kids-brochurenames.pdf#search=%22Parenting%20in%20a%20commercial%20culture%22.

4. Miroslav Volf, *Free of Charge* (Grand Rapids: Zondervan, 2005), 14.

5. Department of Health and Human Services, Federal Register, January 23, 2008 (vol. 73, no. 15), 3971–3972, http://aspe.hhs.gov/POVERTY/08fedreg.htm.

6. Kanaga Raja, "United Nations: No Progress in Reducing Global Hunger," *Social Watch*, June 14, 2007, www.globalpolicy.org/component/content/article/217/46192.html.

7. "Happy 4th Anniversary," Podcast #225, *More Hip than Hippie*, www.morethanhippie.com/index.php?post_id=495541.

8. www.cartalk.com/content/features/carbon/interview.html.

CHAPTER 5: Cotton Onesies and Bamboo Sheets: Eco-Language Lessons

1. http://recipes.howstuffworks.com/food-fillers–101.htm.

2. http://www.leopold.iastate.edu/pubs/staff/files/food_travel072103.pdf.

3. Penn, Schoen and Berland Associates Press, "Consumers Will Double Spending on Green: Green Brands Survey 2.5," September 27, 2007, www.psbresearch.com/press_media_sept28-2007.htm.

4. Edward Iwate, "Companies Turn Up the Green," *USA Today*, January 31, 2008, www.usatoday.com/money/industries/environment/2008-01-30-greenbiz-green-companies_N.htm.

5. CBC News (Canada), "Big Sharks Now Functionally Extinct," March 30, 2007, www.flmnh.ufl.edu/fish/sharks/InNews/extinct2007.html.

6. Gary Nabham, "The Beginning and the End of the Colorado River: Protecting the Sources, Ensuring Its Courses," www.garynabhan.com/press/gpn000021 .html.

CHAPTER 6: Green House: Making the Changes That Work for Your Family

1. Doris Christopher, "Reclaiming the Family Table for a Balanced Life" (lecture, Christ Church of Oak Brook, Oak Brook, Ill., May 14, 2008).

2. From the wrapper of Seventh Generation Bath Tissue, www.seventhgen eration.com.

CHAPTER 8: Working the System: Purchasing Power

1. www.globalexchange.org/campaigns/fairtrade/cocoa/IITACocoaResearch. pdf. Page 16.

2. http://money.cnn.com/2008/01/24/news/international/chocolate_bitter sweet.fortune/

3. Richard Swift, "Chocolate Saves the World," *The New Internationalist,* www .newint.org/issue304/conclusion.html.

4. Frances Moore Lappe, *Diet for a Small Planet* (Random House: New York, 1991), p. 69.

5. www.greenrightnow.com/kabc/2009/04/01/food-vs-the-environment -getting-to-the-meat-of-the-problem/

CHAPTER 9: Green Traditions: Celebrating Holidays and Special Days

1. Gertrud Mueller Nelson, *To Dance with God: Family Ritual and Community Celebration* (Mahwah, N.J.: Paulist Press, 1986), 63.

CHAPTER 10: Water Bottles and Jet Fuel: Green on the Go

1. Jeffrey Sachs, *Common Wealth: Economics for a Crowded Planet* (New York: Penguin, 2008), 76.

2. US Census Bureau, Press Release: New York Has Longest Commute to Work in Nation, American Community Survey Finds (February 25, 2004), www.census.gov/Press-Release/www/releases/archives/american_community_ survey_acs/001695.html.

3. US Department of Transportation: Bureau of Transportation Statistics "Top 50 Airports Enplaned on US Carriers: 1996, 2005, and 2006."

CHAPTER 11: Green Worship: Can Your Church Go Green?

1. Philip Yancey, "The God Who Can't Be Tamed," *Christianity Today*, Bible study, November 14, 2007, www.christianitytoday.com/biblestudies/articles/spiritualgrowth/071114.html.

CHAPTER 12: Plant a Tree: Looking Out for Every Mom

1. Jo Kuper and Martin Hojsik, "Poisoning the Poor: Electronic Waste in Ghana," *Greenpeace International*, August 5, 2008, www.greenpeace.org/international/press/reports/poisoning-the-poor-electonic.

2. Kimberley D. Mok, "E-Waste in India: A Growing Industry and Environmental Threat", *Treehugger*, October 9, 2007. www.treehugger.com/files/2007/10/e-waste_in_india.php.

3. Gordon Aeschliman, introduction to the *Green Bible* (San Francisco: HarperOne, 2008), 92.

4. Wangari Maathai, interview by Emily Main, "Establishing Roots: Wangari Maathai," *National Geographic: The Green Room*, October 7, 2008, http://blogs.nationalgeographic.com/blogs/admin/mt-search.cgi?tag=environmentalism&blog_id=61.